MEDICAL ASTROLOGY

Jeffrey Wolf Green

MEDICAL ASTROLOGY

Copyright © 2014 School of Evolutionary Astrology.

All rights reserved.

ISBN-13:978-1533622945

ISBN-10:1533622949

TABLE OF CONTENTS

Chapter 1	Basic Principles of EA chart analysis	1
Chapter2	Astrological correlations to the Anatomy, Physiology, the Chakras ..	6
Chapter 3	Medical Terminology ..	31
Chapter 4	Questions and Answers	42
Chapter 5	Practice Charts	80
Chapter 6	Medical Index	131
Chapter 7	Other EA books, Dvd's, Transcripts, etc	148

ACKNOWLEDGMENTS

Catharine Anderson (Cat)

Patrick Chehab (Skywalker)

Kristin Fontana

Linda Jonson

Katherine Sanders

Adina Mather

Ari Moshe Wolfe

Gonzalo Romero

Upasika

ABOUT THE AUTHOR

Jeffrey Wolf Green has been called the founder of Evolutionary Astrology because he first started to lecture on the revolutionary astrological paradigm in 1977 after receiving a dream from the spiritual master Swami Sri Yukteswar, Paramahansa Yogananda's guru. In that dream the entire paradigm of Evolutionary Astrology was conveyed to Jeffrey. This was the first time in astrology's long history that a specific paradigm was realized that allowed for an understanding of the evolutionary progression of a Soul from life to life. Jeffrey lectured all over the world on Evolutionary Astrology from 1977 to 2001. He established Evolutionary Astrology schools in a number of countries and wrote three books on Evolutionary Astrology.

The first of these, *Pluto: The Evolutionary Journey of the Soul, Volume I* was published in 1984. It has been in continuous print ever since and has become one of the all-time best selling astrology books. Translations have been made into French, German, Dutch, Chinese, Bulgarian, Spanish, Portuguese, Italian, Serbian and other languages. Volume II, *Pluto: The Soul's Evolution through Relationships* was published in 1998 and has been in continuous print. A third volume, *Essays in Evolutionary Astrology: The Evolutionary Journey of the Soul*, was published in 2010. *Essays* was compiled by his daughter Deva Green from transcriptions of workshops Jeffrey gave over the years. It covers topics that are part of Jeffrey's Evolutionary Astrology paradigm that were either not covered in depth or in some cases at all in his original two volumes.

Since starting his original Pluto School in 1994, Jeffrey had many EA students, a number of whom are now professional EA astrologers. He personally counseled over 30,000 clients in his lengthy career. This exposure to so many Souls from so many different backgrounds and orientations allowed him to come to the deepest possible understandings of the nature of the Soul. He communicated these insights through all of his teachings. In 2008 his daughter Deva Green, took over her father's work. She established the Jeffrey Wolf Green School of Evolutionary Astrology website, and created the EA School's Evolutionary Astrology Council who assist Deva with the School's mission of disseminating Jeffrey's original work around the planet.

www.schoolofevolutionaryastrology.com/school/

"A child is born on that day and at that hour when the celestial rays are in mathematical harmony with his or her individual karma. The resulting horoscope is a challenging portrait revealing his or her unalterable past, and its probable future result. But the natal chart can be Rightly interpreted only by women and men of intuitive wisdom: these are few."

SWAMI SRI YUKTESWAR

YOGANNADA AND YUKTESWAR

1 Basic Principles Of EA Chart Analysis

General Medical Astrology

The essence of astrology is a natural science based on correlation and observation. Thus, over thousands of years correlations have been developed that connect to the entire anatomy and physiology of the human body. Once these correlations are understood, it is not all that difficult to understand in any chart what areas within the body may have potential difficulties; ie Saturn squaring Jupiter, for example, in general, can correlate among other things, to a restriction in the sciatic nerves or a very slow metabolism process. The chakra system also has its own correlations. In Western terminology the chakras translate into what are called spinal plexuses.

Combining the two systems can lead to a very precise understanding of the entire body for any given person/birth chart and the psychological reasons for whatever conditions are apparent. We must remember that if we walk up to a corpse and put bread in its mouth, it cannot chew; there must be a consciousness present for it to chew. Thus, the consciousness, psychology, is the determining factor for what is happening in the body.

What is happening in the body is a reflection of the genetic structure that each incarnating Soul 'inherits' from its parents at birth, as the parents, as well as the overall life circumstances, are chosen by the Soul, to promote and facilitate its evolutionary growth, necessities, and karmic issues. Thus, the genetic structure combined with all the prior lives of any Soul that apply to the current life combine in such a way as to determine the total situation of the physical body in any given life.

Some conditions in the body are karmically determined for whatever reasons, and, when this is the case, one of two situations exists:

(1) the condition cannot be healed in the current life no matter what healer does what, or

(2) it is determined for a specific length of time, which itself can be determined by the Soul's ability, willingness, or capacity to understand the actual causes and then to do something about it.

The *potential* for medical issues

All the various astrological symbols, eg Mars, Cancer, the 4th house etc., correlate to all the various anatomical, physiological, and chakra system functions that symbolize the *potential* for medical issues in each of the archetypes. In other words, when we analyze any given symbol, from a medical point of view, the potential exists to have medical issues in those symbols versus some absolute manifestation of a medical issue in those symbols.

We will use that perspective of potential versus an absolutist one. Given the potential in any given astrological symbol, transits and progressions can correlate to the manifestation of that potential at those times. We will also try to understand the inherent genetics, Pluto, Scorpio, and the 8th house, of any given symbol in such a way as to consider how any given Soul can literally be born with medical issues.

Start simply by considering the medical potential of two planets. From there take those same two planets and connect them to signs, and then, from there to houses. As we progress further on we will then begin to add other planets in a building block approach to our medical understanding that will lead to looking at an entire birth chart.

So as we begin examining two planets at first it will simply be a matter of referring to the anatomical, physiological, and chakra system correlations of those two planets.

Aspects

We should also understand that the nature of aspects between planets correlate to the relative probability of having medical issues connected to those planets. In other words, two planets in opposition versus those same two planets in a trine will correlate to an increased probability of having medical issues between those two planets. The aspects also correlate to the potential degree of how severe any given medical issue is between two planets. Again, a trine between two planets not only has a decreased probability of medical issues but also, if they did manifest, a less severe manifestation of them versus those two planets being in an opposition for example.

Root of genetics

The best way to learn about the anatomy and physiology of the body is to see the 'whole' of it first so that all of its individual parts then make sense. That starts with understanding the genetic structure of the body as a root issue. From that root of genetics all manifests from there: like a root of a flower that then creates a stem, branches, and then flowers. The body is just like that. So by understanding the root of genetics all other body things can be understood.

Pluto, Scorpio and the 8th house

We will try to understand the inherent genetics, Pluto, Scorpio, and the 8th house, of any given symbol in such a way as to consider how any given Soul can literally be born with medical issues.

It will simply be a matter of referring to the anatomical, physiological, and chakra system correlations of those two planets.

Planet – sign – house

[Example: Moon – Cancer – 4th house] The Moon and Cancer have their correlations which are not different at all. Where ever you find the Moon in the chart, or the sign Cancer, the correlations are the same. The specific houses and signs that any planet falls within, the archetypal correlations to that planet, are then added onto relative to the archetypal correlations of that house and/or sign. So too with the planetary ruler of a house adding to the core archetypes of the house itself.

STEP 1

[See Chapter 5 – Chart A Practice Charts]

Examine the correlations that have been provided about the anatomy, physiology, and the chakra systems and then link those correlations to the example: Mars opposed Uranus. So, in this example we would simply refer to the correlations of Mars, Aries, and the 1st house to the correlations of Uranus, Aquarius, and the 11th house and put that in the context of an opposition. There is no need to read medical books.

STEP 2

[See Chapter 5 — Chart B Practice Charts]

The next step is to place the Uranus/Mars opposition in a specific house. So let's put Uranus in the 4th house, and Mars in the 10th. When you refer to the correlations that have been provided focus on the sign Cancer and the 4th house, and Saturn and the 10th house. These houses now correlate to not only the type of inner and outer conditions that can serve to ignite the inherent potentialities of the Mars opposed Uranus, but also add to what those potentialities may be as defined by the houses that this aspect takes place within.

STEP 3

[See Chapter 5 — Chart C Practice Charts]

The next step will be to put the Uranus/Mars opposition in the 4th/10th houses in a sign to determine additional psychological/ medical correlations: to see if in so doing there are more **potential** issues that may occur. We will put Uranus in Virgo, and Mars in Pisces. What additional potentials could exist in so doing?

2 ASTROLOGICAL CORRELATIONS (PLUTO, SIGNS, HOUSES) TO ANATOMY, PHYSIOLOGY,

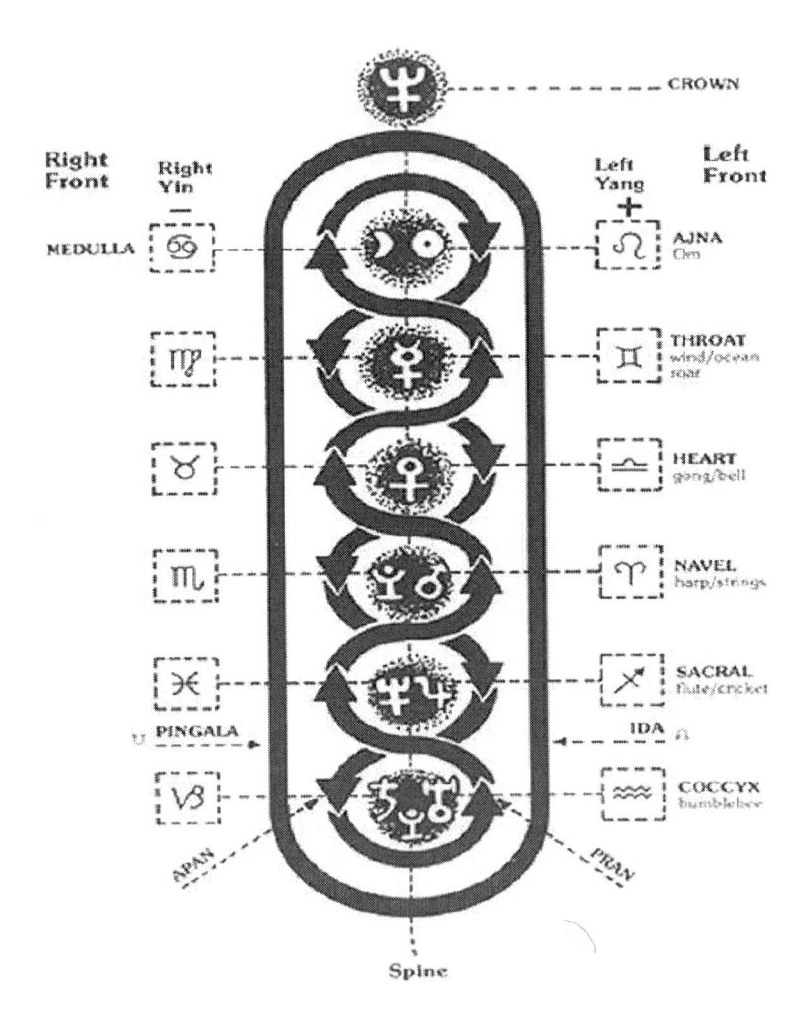

AND THE CHAKRA SYSTEM
Chakra correlations

Mars – Aries – 1st House

Anatomical Correlations – Mars

- Adrenal glands with Venus and Pluto
- Arteries with Pluto and Saturn
- Duodenum which is co-ruled with Pluto
- Muscles and muscular tissues of all kinds
- Oesophagus which is co-ruled with Pluto
- Penis with Pluto
- Primary brain which is co-ruled with the Moon and Pluto
- Red blood cells with Pluto
- Testes with Pluto
- Veins with Pluto and Saturn

Physiological Correlations – Mars

- Acetylcholine with Uranus
- Acids (all acids) in the body with Pluto
- Adrenaline
- Luteinizing hormone with Pluto
- Pregnenolone
- Progesterone
- Testosterone

Chakra System Correlations – Mars

Naval chakra with Pluto

Venus – Taurus – 2nd House

Anatomical Correlations – Venus

- Adrenal glands which are co-ruled with Mars and Pluto
- Frontal lobes and the parietal lobes which are co-ruled with Uranus and Neptune
- Inner brain with Neptune and Uranus
- Kidneys with Pluto and Neptune
- Nose with Saturn
- Receptor cells throughout the body
- Receptors in the brain with Uranus and Neptune
- Spleen with Pluto and Neptune
- Tongue
- White blood cells

Physiological Correlations – Venus

- Adrenocorticotrophic hormone (ACTH) with co-ruler Jupiter.
- Corticotrophin-releasing hormone, or CRH (controls ACTH release) with Jupiter.
- Hydrocortisone hormones, also known as cortisol, controls the body's use of fats, proteins and carbohydrates.
- Corticosterone which, together with cortisol, suppresses inflammatory reactions in the body and also has an effect on the immune system with Saturn.
- Estrogen with Pluto.

Chakra System Correlations – Venus

Heart chakra

Additional Correlations – Venus

Additionally, Venus, Taurus, and the 2nd house correlates to all the various 'senses' – 'sensing' within the body – which are co-ruled with Neptune and Pluto. These also correlate with extremes that can exist in the body that then need to be balanced as a result: thus the sense of balance with the body. These also correlate with the psychology of hearing: how we hear.

Mercury – Gemini – 3rd House

Anatomical Correlations – Mercury

- Amygdala with the Moon, Pluto, and Uranus
- Anatomy of the ear
- Arms and hands
- Entire central Nervous system with co-ruler Uranus
- Left hemisphere: with Uranus
- Motor nerves
- Neurotransmitters with Uranus and Neptune
- Sciatic nerves with co-ruler Uranus and Jupiter
- Sympathetic and parasympathetic systems with co-rulers the Moon and Uranus*
- Temporal lobe with Uranus

*The nervous system is made up of the Central Nervous System (CNS) and the Peripheral Nervous System (PNS). Comprised of neural and nervous tissue, the CNS and PNS transmit signals from the brain to the body parts (muscles, glands, sense organs) to activate a response which correlates with co-rulers Uranus and Pluto.

Chakra System Correlations – Mercury

Throat chakra

Additional Correlations – Mercury

With co-ruler Uranus it correlates with the very nature of thought: thinking. As a result it correlates with the 'messaging' taking place within the entire physical body that is ultimately traceable to the various areas within the brain itself.

Additionally, Mercury with Uranus correlates to all the transmissions within the body that all involve the body communicating with itself. Additionally, this correlates with all the external transmissions that come into the body that impacts on how the body reacts to those transmissions. In combination these then correlate to how the body, and the Soul within it, transmits or communicates itself to others specifically, and the overall environment generally.

Moon – Cancer – 4th House

Anatomical Correlations – Moon

- Eyes, optical nerve, retina, and the pupil
- Stomach with co-ruler Pluto
- Primary brain co-ruled with Uranus and Mars
- Breasts co-ruled with Pluto
- Midbrain with Uranus
- Occipital lobe with Uranus
- Limbic system with Neptune and Pluto as general co-rulers
- Amygdala with Uranus, Pluto, and Mercury
- Cingulate gyrus with Uranus
- Hypothalamus with Uranus and Neptune
- Ovaries with Pluto
- Vagina with Pluto
- Uterus with Pluto
- Bladder
- Sympathetic and parasympathetic systems with co-rulers Uranus and Mercury.
- Placenta with Neptune and Pluto.
- Umbilical cord with Neptune and Pluto.
- Mucous membranes, the lubricating membrane lining an internal surface or organ, eg gums, stomach, etc. which correlate with Pluto.
- Serous membrane: thin membranes that line cavities that secrete serous fluid, eg peritoneum with co-ruler Pluto.
- Loose connective tissue: including adipose tissue (fat storage) which correlates with Saturn and Pluto.
- Smooth muscular tissue in the eye.

Physiological Correlations – Moon

- Anti-diuretic hormone (ADH) with co-rulers Neptune and Jupiter.
- Breast milk.
- Follicle-stimulating hormone (FSH) with co-ruler Jupiter.
- Neurotransmitter serotonin which is co-ruled with Saturn.
- Prolactin: stimulates milk production from a woman's breasts after childbirth. In pregnant and breastfeeding women, prolactin helps prevent ovulation (the release of eggs from the ovaries): with Jupiter.
- Water with Pluto and Neptune.

Chakra System Correlations – Moon

Third eye chakra with Pluto

Sun – Leo – 5th House

Anatomical Correlations – Sun

- Cardiovascular system: circulation of the blood.
- Heart as an organ with co-ruler Mars because of the cardiac muscle tissue that it is composed of.

Chakra System Correlation – Sun

Third eye or ajna co-ruled with Moon and Pluto.

The ajna chakra is actually linked to the medulla and the crown chakra to form a natural triangle. When a Soul is able to open this ajna chakra it then begins to perceive the inner cosmos, the very nature of Creation including the creation of itself and all others. This perception within the ajna is projected by way of the medulla wherein lies the seat of the Soul itself, and the ego, Moon, that it creates in each life. As the progressive perception takes place within the ajna of the inner cosmos, of that which has created All Things, a natural shift in the very gravity of consciousness occurs: from the ego to the Soul itself. As this evolves this then ignites the crown chakra itself which is ruled by Neptune.

Additional Correlations – Sun

Additionally, the Sun, Leo, and the 5th house correlate to the overall vitality of the body, and directly correlates to the temperature of the body.

Mercury – Virgo – 6th House

Anatomical Correlations – Mercury

- Amygdala with the Moon, Pluto, and Uranus
- Anatomy of the ear
- Arms and hands
- Entire central Nervous system with co-ruler Uranus
- Left hemisphere: with Uranus
- Motor nerves
- Neurotransmitters with Uranus and Neptune
- Sciatic nerves with co-ruler Uranus and Jupiter
- Sympathetic and parasympathetic systems with co-rulers the Moon and Uranus*
- Temporal lobe with Uranus
-

*The nervous system is made up of the Central Nervous System (CNS) and the Peripheral Nervous System (PNS). Comprised of neural and nervous tissue, the CNS and PNS transmit signals from the brain to the body parts (muscles, glands, sense organs) to activate a response which correlates with co-rulers Uranus and Pluto.

Chakra System Correlation – Mercury

Throat chakra

Additional Correlations – Mercury

With co-ruler Uranus it correlates with the very nature of thought: thinking. As a result it correlates with the 'messaging' taking place within the entire physical body that is ultimately traceable to the various areas within the brain itself. Additionally, Mercury with Uranus correlates to all the transmissions within the body that all involve the body communicating with itself. Additionally, this correlates with all the external transmissions that come into the body that impacts on how the body reacts to those transmissions. In combination these then correlate to how the body, and the Soul within it, transmits or communicates itself to others specifically, and the overall environment generally.

Venus – Libra – 7th House

Anatomical Correlations – Venus

- Adrenal glands which are co-ruled with Mars and Pluto
- Frontal lobes and the parietal lobes which are co-ruled with Uranus and Neptune
- Inner brain with Neptune and Uranus
- Kidneys with Pluto and Neptune
- Nose with Saturn
- Receptor cells throughout the body
- Receptors in the brain with Uranus and Neptune
- Spleen with Pluto and Neptune
- Tongue
- White blood cells

Physiological Correlations – Venus

- Adrenocorticotrophic hormone (ACTH) with co-ruler Jupiter.
- Corticotrophin-releasing hormone, or CRH (controls ACTH release) with Jupiter.
- Hydrocortisone hormones, also known as cortisol, controls the body's use of fats, proteins and carbohydrates.
- Corticosterone which, together with cortisol, suppresses inflammatory reactions in the body and also has an effect on the immune system with Saturn.
- Estrogen with Pluto.

Chakra System Correlations – Venus

Heart chakra

Additional Correlations – Venus

Additionally, Venus, Taurus, and the 2nd house correlates to all the various 'senses' – 'sensing' within the body – which are co-ruled with Neptune and Pluto. These also correlate with extremes that can exist in the body that then need to be balanced as a result: thus the sense of balance with the body. These also correlate with the psychology of hearing: how we hear.

Pluto – Scorpio – 8th House

Anatomical Correlations – Pluto

- Anal canal co-ruled with Saturn.
- Arteries co-ruled with Mars and Saturn.
- Blood co-ruled with Mars and Venus (blood is classified as a 'connective tissue' which is why it is listed here as anatomical).
- Brain stem with Uranus and Neptune.
- Breasts co-ruled with the Moon.
- Capillaries co-ruled with Saturn.
- Duodenum co-ruled with Mars.
- Endocrine system and all glands which have different co-rulers depending on specific functions of those glands. For example:
    - pineal gland co-ruled with Neptune,
    - thymus gland co-ruled with Neptune,
    - thyroid gland co-ruled with Jupiter,
    - pituitary gland co-ruled with Saturn and Jupiter,
    - adrenal glands co-ruled with Mars and Venus,
    - parathyroid gland co-ruled with Saturn and Jupiter.
- Esophagus co-ruled with Mars.
- Gallbladder with co-ruler Jupiter where Jupiter correlates with bile.
- Genetic structures of life itself, including humans. Within this to the RNA/DNA chromosomes.
- Kidneys with co-ruler Venus.
- Lymph glands and tonsils co-ruled with Neptune.
- Nucleus within all body cells. Ovaries, uterus, and

vagina in women co-ruled with the Moon, and the testes and penis in men co-ruled with Mars.
- Pancreas and liver co-ruled with Jupiter, and the entire intestinal tract.
- Primary brain co-ruled with the Moon and Mars.
- Prostrate, in men, co-ruled with Jupiter.
- Spinal column co-ruled with Saturn.
- Spleen co-ruled with Venus and Neptune.
- Spleen co-ruled with Venus and Neptune.
- Stomach co-ruled with the Moon.
- Veins co-ruled with Mars and Saturn.

Physiological Correlations – Pluto

- Enzymes (all)
- Feces
- Hormones
- Insulin
- Kundalini
- Sperm in men, and ovum in women
- Spinal fluid
- Toxins (all)
- Urine

Chakra System Correlation – Pluto

Root chakra: its core, co-ruled with Saturn and Uranus

Naval chakra co-ruled with Mars

Additional Correlations – Pluto

These archetypes also correlate with actions within the physical body called mutations, evolution, the formation of cysts, pimples, cancer, tumors of all kinds, purification, regeneration, diseases and infections, eliminations, secretions, death of the body, and giving birth.

bacteria, Mold, parasites, viruses,

Jeffrey Wolf Green Evolutionary Astrology

Additionally, Pluto, Scorpio, and the 8th house correlate to all bacteria, viruses, parasites, and mold. And, most importantly, these archetypes correlate to **ALL THE AMINO ACIDS THAT LEAD TO THE CREATION OF PROTEINS**.

Again, there are many other detailed correlations of Pluto, Scorpio, and the 8th house that cannot be listed here because it would simply be too exhaustive, ie Pluto correlates to mitochondria.

Jupiter – Sagittarius – 9th House

Anatomical Correlations – Jupiter

- Pituitary gland with co-rulers Saturn and Pluto
- Parathyroid gland co-ruled with Pluto and Saturn
- Basal ganglia with Uranus
- Right hemisphere in the brain
- Liver with co-ruler Pluto
- Thyroid gland with co-ruler Pluto
- Sciatic nerves with co-rulers Uranus and Mercury

Physiological Correlations – Jupiter

Hormones of the liver: Angiotensinogen, Thrombopoietin, Hepcidin, and Betatrophin. The liver also naturally produces cholesterol and bile.

Hormones of the thyroid: T4 (thyroxine), T3 (tri-iodothyronine or liothyronine), T2 (di-iodothyronine), and T1 (mono-iodothyronine). These regulate all the processes of energy release within the body's cells.

Hormone secreted from the parathyroid which is PTH.

Hormones of the pituitary co-ruled with Saturn and Pluto in general are:

Anterior Pituitary:

- Adrenocorticotrophic hormone (ACTH) with co-ruler

Venus
- Thyroid-stimulating hormone (TSH)
- Luteinizing hormone (LH)
- Follicle-stimulating hormone (FSH) with co-ruler Moon
- Prolactin (PRL)
- Growth hormone (GH)
- Melanocyte-stimulating hormone (MSH)

Posterior Pituitary: Anti-diuretic hormone (ADH) with co-ruler Moon. Oxytocin with co-ruler Neptune.

Chakra System Correlations – Jupiter

Sacral chakra with co-ruler Neptune

Additional Correlations – Jupiter

Additionally Jupiter correlates with the essential co-ordination of the entire body, and the metabolism of all nutrients that are put into the body. Because of its correlation to growth hormones this can also then lead to out of control growth of anything in the body that then creates its own physical issues and symptoms.

Saturn – Capricorn – 10th House

Anatomical Correlations – Saturn

Entire skeleton with specific co-ruler to different areas of the body:

- Spine co-ruled with Pluto
- Arms and hands with Mercury
- Neck with Venus
- Head with Mars
- Feet with Neptune
- Legs with Jupiter
- Pelvis with Pluto
- Teeth
- Anal canal with Pluto
- Skin with co-ruler Neptune as this correlates with the pigmentation in the skin relative to the hormone melanin.
- Bone marrow and the B and T cells that emanate from it.
- Sheathing within the nerves called myelin.
- Cortex with Uranus
- Fornix with Uranus
- Parahippocampal gyrus with Uranus
- Pituitary gland co-ruled with Jupiter and Pluto
- Parathyroid gland co-ruled with Jupiter and Pluto
- Cell structure
- Cutaneous membrane which pertains to the skin which correlates with Saturn.

- Synovia membrane which pertains to dense connective tissue that secretes synovial fluid which correlates with co-ruler Pluto.
- Cartilage tissues with co-ruler Pluto.
- Muscle tissue that connects to the skeletal bones co-ruled with Mars
- Trachea co-ruled with Uranus
- Structure of the nose co-ruled with Uranus and Venus
- Valves within the body including the valves within the heart

Physiological Correlations – Saturn

- Spinal fluid co-ruled with Pluto
- Synovial fluids
- Fats

Chakra System Correlations – Saturn

Outer layer of the root chakra co-ruled with Uranus, the middle layer, and Pluto to the core.

Additional Correlations – Saturn

Additionally Saturn correlates with the aging of the body, to deposits of various kinds, to crystallization of various kinds, to atrophy, to arthritis, to decay, restrictions of various kinds within the body, and the overall structural integrity of the whole of the physical body.

Uranus – Aquarius – 11th House

Anatomical Correlations – Uranus

Brain in general with specific co-rulers:

- Hindbrain or primary brain with Pluto
- Midbrain: with the Moon
- Inner brain: with Venus and Neptune
- Left hemisphere with Mercury
- Right hemisphere with Jupiter
- Cortex with Saturn
- Frontal lobes and the parietal lobes co-ruled with Venus and Neptune
- Occipital lobe with the Moon
- Temporal lobe with Mercury
- Brain stem with Neptune and Pluto

Within the brain:

Medulla

- Limbic system with Neptune, Moon, and Pluto as general co-rulers
- Amygdala with the Moon, Pluto, and Mercury
- Cingulate gyrus with the Moon
- Fornix with Saturn
- Parahippocampal gyrus with Saturn
- Hypothalamus with the Moon
- Thalamus with Neptune

- Hippocampus
- Basal ganglia with Jupiter
- Synapses
- Neurons
- Axons
- Sacs
- Receptors with Venus and Neptune
- Sheath that can have myelin within it that is then co-ruled with Saturn.

Neurotransmitters with Mercury and Neptune in general with specific correlations like Acetylcholine that is then co-ruled with Mars, GABA co-ruled with Saturn, and Serotonin co-ruled with Saturn and the Moon.

Physiological Correlations – Uranus

The types of neurotransmitters also correlate with specific physiological substances:

- Dopamine
- Serotonin
- Gaba
- Acetylcholine

Additional Anatomical Correlations – Uranus

- Entire central nervous system with co-ruler Mercury
- Sympathetic and parasympathetic systems with co-rulers the Moon and Mercury
- Sheathing on the various nerves throughout the body co-ruled with Saturn
- Lungs and bronchial tubes
- Trachea co-ruled with Saturn
- Structure of the nose co-ruled with Saturn and Venus

- **Chakra System Correlations – Uranus**

Mid layer of the root chakra, the outer layer co-ruled with Saturn, the core co-ruled with Pluto. With the co-ruler Mercury it correlates with the very nature of thought: thinking. As a result it correlates with the 'messaging' taking place within the entire physical body that is ultimately traceable to the various areas within the brain itself.

Uranus also correlates with what are called 'free radicals,' strokes, dehydration, stress and tension, and the full spectrum of neurological disorders. It also correlates to the physical action of 'bursting' when an existing restriction within the body has reached an extreme that then triggers this bursting action.

Neptune – Pisces – 12th House

Anatomical Correlations – Neptune

Pineal gland with Pluto

- Thymus gland with Pluto and the hormone called thymosin
- B and T cells with Saturn
- Immune system in general with specific co-rulers depending on other functions in the body that correlate with immunity. For example, with Pluto because of its correlation with the intestinal tract.
- Feet
- Spleen co-ruled with Pluto and Venus

Physiological Correlations – Neptune

- Melatonin
- Serotonin
- Melanin
- All fluids in the body with co-rulers Pluto and the Moon
- Dopamine

Chakra System Correlations – Neptune

Crown chakra

- Sacral chakra with co-ruler Jupiter
- Astral body

Additional Correlations – Neptune

(handwritten: 4 Consciousness of the Soul)

MEDICAL ASTROLOGY

Neptune also correlates with the phenomena of consciousness, the consciousness of the Soul. It correlates with sleep/being awake, dreams, visions, and hallucinations that occur within consciousness.

3 MEDICAL TERMINOLOGY

Tissues Of The Human Body

A layer or group of cells that collectively perform a specific function forms tissues. These are the main types of tissues found in the human body and their functions. Tissues are composed of groups or layers of cells, which collectively perform a specific function. Different types of tissues have different structures that are specific to their function. Tissues can be held together by a sticky coating called an 'extracellular matrix' or the matrix may weave the cells of tissues together. The Latin word for tissue is derived from the verb texere, "to weave." These are the major tissue types in the human body:

- Connective
- Epithelial
- Muscular
- Nervous system
- Lymphatic

Connective tissue

Connective tissue is made up of cells and protein fibers and provides support for other body tissues. The main proteins in connective tissue are collagen and elastin. There are five types of connective tissue. They are:

- Loose connective tissue: including adipose tissue (fat storage) which correlates with the Moon and Pluto
- Dense connective tissue which correlates with Pluto

- Blood which correlates with Mars, Venus and Pluto
- Bone which correlates with Pluto and Saturn
- Cartilage which correlates with Pluto and Saturn

Epithelial tissue

Epithelial tissue, often called epithelium, is comprised of tightly packed cells, arranged to form layers. Epithelium provides many functions, including absorption, excretion, protection, reproduction, secretion and sensory reception. Epithelial cells are constantly renewing and replacing the dead or inactive cells. The two main epithelial tissue types are:

- Glandular: found in exocrine and endocrine glands which correlates with Pluto
- Lining epithelium: forms the outer layer of the skin and in some internal organs which correlates with Pluto and Saturn

Muscular tissue

Muscle tissue provides stability to the skeleton and internal organs and allows body movement. Muscle tissue makes up approximately 60% of the body's mass and there are three types of muscle tissue. These are:

- Cardiac: found in the heart which correlates with the Sun, Mars, and Pluto
- Skeletal: usually attached to bone which correlates with Pluto, Mars, and Saturn
- Smooth: found in walls of blood vessels in digestive system, respiratory system and the eye which correlates with Pluto, Uranus, and the Moon respectively.

Nervous system tissue

The nervous system is made up of the Central Nervous

System (CNS) and the Peripheral Nervous System (PNS). Comprised of neural and nervous tissue, the CNS and PNS transmit signals from the brain to the body parts (muscles, glands, sense organs) to activate a response which correlates with Uranus, Mercury, and Pluto.

Lymphatic tissue

Lymphatic, or lymphoid tissue is found at the entrance of the digestive system, respiratory system and urogenital tracts. The lymphoid tissue provides protection as a first line of defense for these areas which correlates with Neptune and Pluto.

MEMBRANES

Membranes are thin layers of tissue that provide a surface lining or protective surface to organs or body structures. There are four types of membranes. They are:

- Cutaneous: pertaining to the skin which correlates with Saturn.
- Mucous: the lubricating membrane lining an internal surface or organ. An example of mucous membrane would be the gums which correlate with the Moon and Pluto.
- Serous: thin membranes that line cavities that secrete serous fluid. An example would be the peritoneum which correlates with Pluto and the Moon.
- Synovial: dense connective tissue membrane that secretes synovial fluid correlating with Pluto and Saturn.

ENDOCRINE SYSTEM AND HORMONES

The endocrine system and the hormones they secrete:

- Hypothalamus
- Pituitary
- Pineal
- Thyroid
- Para-thyroid
- Adrenal
- Thymus
- Pancreas (partly gland, partly organ)
- Gonads (ovaries and testes)

Hypothalamus: Uranus, Moon, and Neptune

The hypothalamus is part of the brain that lies just above the pituitary gland. It releases hormones that start and stop the release of pituitary hormones. The hypothalamus controls hormone production in the pituitary gland through several "releasing" hormones. These include:

- Growth hormone-releasing hormone, or GHRH (controls GH release): Jupiter
- Tyrotropin-releasing hormone, or TRH (controls TSH release): Jupiter
- Corticotrophin-releasing hormone, or CRH (controls ACTH release): Venus

Another hormone made by the hypothalamus is gonadotropin-releasing hormone (GnRH). It tells the pituitary gland to make luteinizing hormone (LH) and follicle-stimulating hormone (FSH), which are important for normal puberty and reproduction: Pluto.

Pituitary: Pluto, Saturn, and Jupiter

- Prolactin: stimulates milk production from a woman's breasts after childbirth. In pregnant and breastfeeding women, prolactin helps prevent ovulation (the release of eggs from the ovaries): Moon.
- Growth hormone (GH): GH stimulates growth in childhood and is important for maintaining a healthy body composition. In adults it is also important for maintaining muscle mass and bone mass. GH also affects fat distribution in the body: Jupiter.
- Adrenocorticotropin (ACTH): ACTH stimulates production of cortisol by the adrenal glands. Cortisol, a so-called "stress hormone," is vital to survival. It helps maintain blood pressure and blood glucose levels, among other effects: Venus.
- Thyroid-stimulating hormone (TSH): TSH stimulates the thyroid gland to make thyroid hormones, which, in turn, control (regulate) the body's metabolism, energy, growth and development, and nervous system activity: Jupiter.
- Luteinizing hormone (LH): LH regulates testosterone in men and estrogen in women: Pluto and Mars.
- Follicle-stimulating hormone (FSH): FSH stimulates the ovaries to release eggs (ovulate) in women: Pluto and the Moon. LH and FSH work together to allow normal function of the ovaries or testes, including sperm production.
- Posterior pituitary (back part of the pituitary) produces two hormones: Oxytocin. Oxytocin causes milk to be released in nursing mothers and contractions during childbirth: Moon. Antidiuretic hormone (ADH): ADH, also called vasopressin, regulates water balance. If ADH is not secreted in the right amount, this can lead to too much or too little sodium (salt) and water in the bloodstream: Neptune.

Pineal: Pluto and Neptune

Melatonin and serotonin which is a precursor for melatonin: Neptune.

Thyroid: Jupiter and Pluto
The thyroid produces two hormones, T3 (called tri-iodothyronine) and T4 (called thyroxine): Jupiter.

Parathyroid: Saturn, Jupiter, and Pluto
PTH: Saturn.

Adrenals: Pluto, Mars, and Venus

The adrenal glands consist of two parts, the cortex or outer portion and the medulla, the inner portion. The adrenal cortex (the outer portion) releases:

- Corticosteroid hormones: Hydrocortisone hormones, also known as cortisol, controls the body's use of fats, proteins and carbohydrates: Venus; Corticosterone which, together with cortisol, suppresses inflammatory reactions in the body and also has an effect on the immune system: Venus.
- Aldosterone hormone which inhibits the level of sodium excreted into the urine, maintaining blood volume and blood pressure: Saturn.
- Androgenic steroids (androgen hormones) which have a minimal effect on the development of male characteristics: Saturn.
- Dehydroepiandrosterone: The main function of DHEA in our body is to work as a precursor for men and women's sex hormones which are described as androgen and estrogen: Pluto.
- Pregnenolone is the precursor hormone from which stress hormones are made, making its presence in

your body significant: Mars.

- Adrenal medulla (the inner portion of the adrenals) releases: Epinephrine (also called adrenaline) increases the heart rate and force of the heart contractions, facilitates blood flow to the muscles and brain, causes relaxation of smooth muscles, helps with conversion of glycogen to glucose in the liver – plus other activities: Mars. Norepinephrine (also called noradrenaline) has strong vasoconstrictive (vaso = blood vessel and constrictive = constriction) effects, thus increasing blood pressure: Saturn.

Thymus: Neptune and Pluto

Humoral factors: Neptune

Pancreas: Pluto

Insulin and glucagon: Pluto

Testes: Pluto and Mars

Testosterone: Pluto and Mars

Ovaries: Pluto and Moon

Estrogen: Pluto and Venus

Progesterone. Pluto and Mars

PRIMARY BRAIN

The two pictures attached show the whole of the primary or hindbrain where the primary brain has the number one on it in the first picture, and the purple color for it in the second picture. Our correlations apply to the WHOLE of the primary brain.

The hindbrain is located toward the rear and lower portion of a person's brain. It is responsible for controlling a number of important body functions and process, including respiration and heart rate. The brain stem is an important part of the hindbrain, and it controls functions that are critical to life, such as breathing and swallowing. The cerebellum is also located here, playing a role in physical ability.

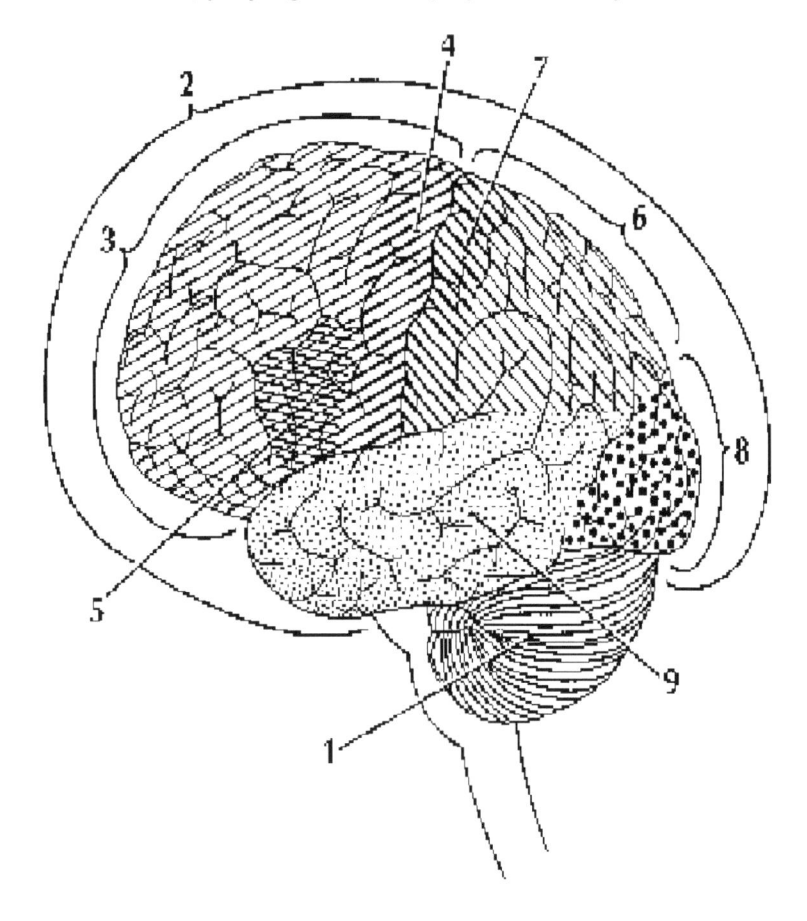

Human brain zones

The brain stem is a structure that connects the brain to the spinal cord. Damage to this structure can be catastrophic, as it controls such things as blood pressure, heartbeat, and swallowing. It is made up of three parts: the medulla, reticular formation, and pons.

The medulla controls how and when a person's heart beats, as well as his blood pressure, breathing, and even his ability to swallow or cough. This part of a person's brain stem functions by itself, without relying on the person's intentions, which is why a person's heart beats without him making it do so. It's also the reason people breathe even when they are focused on other things.

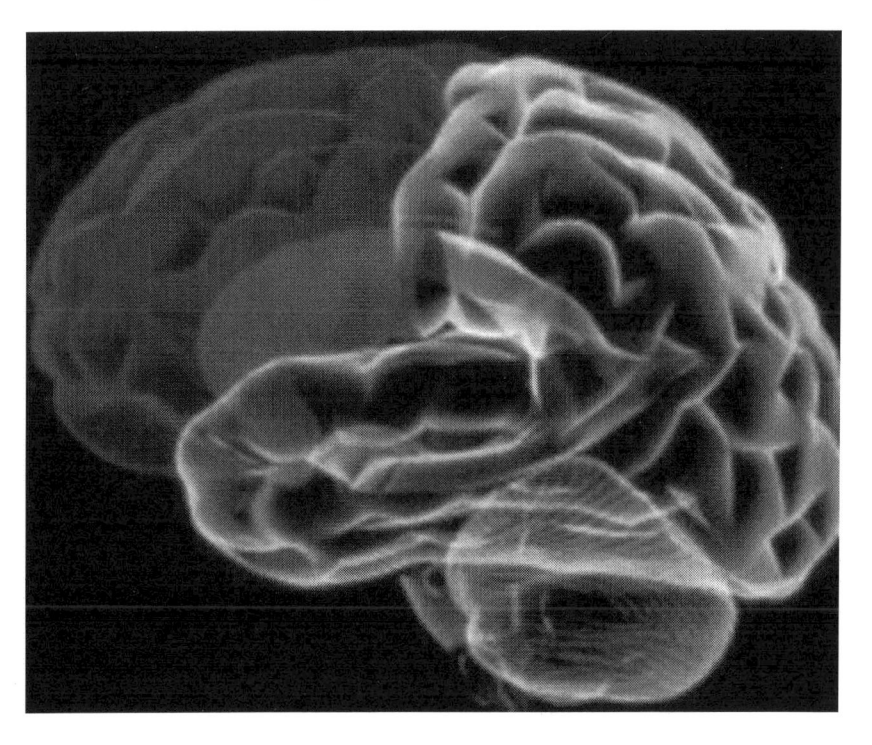

Human brain zones

The reticular formation is a network of nerves important to a person's attention or focus, as well as his response to stimuli. This part of the brain helps an individual pay attention to just one important thing, even if he's faced with several types of stimuli at once. It blocks those less important stimuli, allowing the person to focus. For example, if a person is a potentially dangerous situation, the reticular formation blocks other stimuli, allowing him to focus solely on doing what's needed to help him survive.

Interestingly, the reticular formation slows down when a person goes to sleep. It does not, however, stop working to block some sensory messages while allowing others through. This area of the brain is the reason many people can stay asleep despite the sounds of passing cars or creaks and groans of a house settling, yet wake to the sound of a smoke detector.

The pons is the part of the hindbrain located above the medulla. It forms a kind of bridge between the medulla and the cerebellum. This structure relays messages between the cerebellum and the cerebrum, which is part of the forebrain. It also helps control movement and plays a role in sleep.

The cerebellum is located to the rear of the brain stem. Its role involves muscle tone and posture, influences motor control, and helps a person to perform smooth, controlled movements. The cerebellum also important in coordinating the movements that people make without thinking or concentrating first, such as walking forward.

NERVE COMPLEXES – Uranus and Pluto

The vagus nerve, a cranial nerve running from the medulla down into the organ systems. The "tone" of this nerve has been implicated in a lot of trauma recovery and response, as well as overall emotional regulation and specifically with the capacity to move out of primitive states of mind into more evolved states of mind. The nerve specifically has two parts:

Dorsal vagal complex: The dorsal branch of the vagus

originates in the dorsal motor nucleus and is considered the phylogenetically older branch. This branch is unmyelinated and exists in most vertebrates. This branch is also known as the "vegetative vagus" because it is associated with primal survival strategies of primitive vertebrates, reptiles, and amphibians. Under great stress, these animals freeze when threatened, conserving their metabolic resources.

Ventral vagal complex: With increased neural complexity seen in mammals (due to phylogenetic development) evolved a more sophisticated system to enrich behavioral and affective responses to an increasingly complex environment. The ventral branch of the vagus originates in the nucleus ambiguus and is myelinated to provide more control and speed in responding. This branch is also known as the "smart vagus" because it is associated with the regulation of sympathetic "fight or flight" behaviors in the service of social affiliative behaviors. These behaviors include social communication and self-soothing and calming. In other words, this branch of the vagus can inhibit or disinhibit defensive limbic circuits, depending on the situation. The VVC provides primary control of supradiaphragmatic visceral organs, such as the esophagus, bronchi, pharynx, and larynx. The VVC also exerts important influence on the heart.

4 Questions and Answers

Abortion

(Q): What would be the signature in the chart of a woman who is carrying a lot of guilt from an abortion in the current lifetime? Would you look at planets and signs in and corresponding to the fourth, fifth and eighth houses, as related to the sign Virgo?

(A): There are many potential signatures for that, and the ones you have mentioned certainly apply.

Allopathic antidepressants

(Q1): What is your opinion about the Prozac type antidepressants? My impression of them is that they seem to help with getting out of security-driven (Pluto) behaviors. I am wondering if they blunt the inner, intuitive voice. Are there some instances where you think they are beneficial, perhaps short-term treatment to sort of "get out of the hole?"

(A): To me, they are like putting a band aid on a wound; they don't deal with the causes of the problem, they only attempt to control or minimize it. Prozac can have pretty severe side effects for some. Remember when George Bush, the father of George W. Bush, was president, and he vomited all over himself and the Japanese Premier while on a state visit? And then he passed out right in front of everyone? He was using Prozac then. For some others it can actually induce a state of psychosis, and yet for others it can do the control job it is meant to do. It all depends on one's nature and biochemistry. Yes, Prozac controls or impacts on the levels of serotonin in the brain, which is critical in terms of our emotional states and reality, so Prozac tends to try to find the most stable and 'dull' state emotionally for a person, and thus blunts a lot of the normal functions of the brain and emotions, including one's imaginative or intuitive side.

(Q2): In relation to this question about antidepressants, with specific reference to Prozac, since 5-HTP is a precursor to serotonin, could that be used instead, at least in cases that were not labeled clinical depression? It seems that the medical profession has now moved beyond labeling women with PMS and is now telling many of them that they suffer from PMDD (Pre-Menstrual Dysphoric Disorder), and they are prescribing Sarafem, which is just Prozac by a different name. Would the 5-HTP alone accomplish the same thing? (for those who are not willing or able to realize the underlying causes of this 'problem' in the first place. i.e.. what has been projected on them about women for thousands of years)? Or would it need to be taken in conjunction with something else for this specific 'problem'?

(A): For the general purpose of restoring the natural levels of serotonin within the brain 5-HTP is an excellent product, plus it is natural.. There you can actually read the medical research on this compound, its uses, and dosages. Relative to specific conditions one would need to know what the condition(s) are to actually treat them in the correct way.

Anal canal – Saturn

First, the anal canal is co-ruled with Pluto where Pluto correlates with elimination and feces. Saturn because of its correlations with valves, the anal canal have valves within it, that secrete lubrications to moisten the feces itself that helps in the passage of the feces.

Arthritis

(Q): Is the signature for arthritis and osteoporosis Saturn square Mars? Is the square the only signature, or could it result from any contact?

(A): That can be one of many potential signatures. Both conditions are Saturn, Capricorn, 10th house archetypes, with a decreasing amount of synovial fluids being the cause for the arthritis and a progressive lack of calcium and magnesium for the other, this being caused by a lack of estrogen.

Asthma

(Q): Do you happen to know any herbal treatments for someone with chronic asthma? A friend is seeing a Chinese doctor, and she is prescribing a tea made of dried earthworms. Do you have any ideas on this?

(A): Lung Formula (available at School of EA) is a very powerful, natural medicine for the lungs for all kinds of conditions, including asthma. It is made of four things: the herbs hyssop, mullein, and Echinacea, which are combined with an extract of garlic.

(Q): Can you give us directions on how to make the lung formula?

(A): Use equal parts of the dried herbs (Echinacea, hyssop and mullein) to fill a quart jar half full, then add olive (or vegetable) oil to fill up the rest of the jar and place a lid on it.

Soak the herbs for two weeks and then strain. Separately, simmer a clove of diced garlic in olive oil for approximately 30 minutes so that you have an herb oil and a garlic oil.

Then you mix, for example, 3/4 cup of herb oil with 1/4 cup of garlic oil and place it in a dark jar and refrigerate it. It will last for a long time - up to two years. The dosage is 25 drops a day, 3 times a day, on the tongue.

Bipolar correlations

(Q): Is a strong Gemini signature/stellium, especially if receiving hard aspects, one indicator of a potential for bipolar or manic-depressive psychological conditions (Gemini's association with the twins)? I've been seeing this in a few charts I've been looking at lately, and that's been the case in each. In all of these cases Saturn and Moon are heavily aspected within that Gemini signature as well, through opposition or conjunction. So then, would part of this be that dual or mixed messages (sometimes highly negative, sometimes highly positive - Gemini duality) be a contributing factor to the duality in the person's own psychological orientation? Obviously, I realize there are a lot of factors and signatures that could contribute and that you have to play astrological detective to understand the evolutionary reasons the Soul creates these conditions, but I just wondered if this Gemini signature was one particular marker.

(A): Yes, this can indicate such a disorder because the right brain, which is Jupiter, Sagittarius, ninth house, is constantly 'pulling' the left brain, Mercury, Gemini, third house, towards it in order to compensate (Jupiter) for the heavy gravity in the left brain, which when compresses thru such a signature and creates a maze of competing thoughts and perspectives, etc., resulting in the drive to 'collect' even more information

MEDICAL ASTROLOGY

because of this, which then just complicates the dynamics further: clarity leading to confusion and vice versa.

The right brain tries to create a 'foundation' of one conceptual system of thought to serve as a continuous and consistent way to integrate the maze of thought/information coming in, so that mental/philosophical, and thus emotional stability can be achieved. When Saturn is involved, this is the specific archetype for manic-depression or a progressive psychology of self-defeat. Because Gemini is part of the triad of Libra and Aquarius, the Libra connection, via Aquarius, can also cause multiple personality disorders, which are now called dissociative behaviors.

Blood Sugar (Sanicle)

(A): Which planets/signs correlate to the body's blood sugar level, and where one would look in a chart to find indication of excessively high or low blood sugar? Also, is there a natural remedy for either condition?

(A): Yes, this is always a Pluto, Scorpio, or eighth house problem because of its direct linkage or correlation to the pancreas, which is regulating the levels of sugar in the system relative to insulin. The antidote is an herb called Sanicle, which must be prepared as a tincture. In that form the dosage is 25 eye drops on the tongue, three times a day.

Calc/phos

(Q): The homeopathic remedy you recommend for triggering production of synovial fluid in the joint capsules is Calc/Phos. Is the full name for this one Calcarea Phosphorica?

(A): Yes, I think so. Mag/phos is also good for this.

Colitis (Sanicle, catnip)

(Q): I was going over the medical astrology again and see that colitis correlates to Pluto specifically. Could we also implicate Virgo in the equation and, if so, is there a greater tendency for colitis in the Pluto in Virgo generation? Finally, what natural remedies do you recommend with clients with this problem?

(A): Virgo correlates specifically to the 'tonality' of the colon and intestine, the peristaltic action. The best herb to recreate the tonality/peristaltic action is, believe it or not, catnip. The specific herb/tincture for colitis is sanicle.

Dyslexia

When this occurs within a Soul there is their own individual evolutionary/ karmic need that is unique to each Soul. In other words, I do not see it as a general phenomenon that correlates to some evolutionary development for the entire human species. So from an evolutionary astrology point of view the issue then becomes determining what the individual evolutionary/ karmic need is for a Soul to manifest any degree of dyslexia.

Eczema

(Q): What do you recommend as treatment to clients who have eczema?

(A): Homeopathically gelsemium, tinctures of sanicle and Fo-ti, niacin (the flush kind), Vitamin B complex, and antothenic acid. Nutritionally, I recommend lots and lots of water and having one's primary food intake be grains, green and yellow vegetables and minimizing the intake of meat, although organic meat once a week is a good idea because of the specific enzyme that the body needs that can only be found in meat.

(Q): Do you make correlations between skin disorders and excessive worry, depression, and/or neurological disorders?

(A): Yes.

(Q): Have you seen a significant number of clients with stressed out Saturn/Mercury having skin problems?

(A): Yes, and also with Mercury in the 10th house or in Capricorn.

Electrolytes

They correlate with Uranus because electrolytes are electrically charged, which means that they can conduct electrical impulses. The body needs electrical impulses to make muscle cells contract. The generation of an electrical impulse by a cell requires an electrical voltage to be maintained across the membrane of that cell. The difference in electrolyte levels creates and maintains these electrical voltages.

When the body intakes minerals from food they dissolve into a fluid that is then called an electrolyte. They're present in blood, urine, in the fluid inside the body's cells and in the fluid in the space surrounding the cells. Sodium, calcium, chloride, magnesium and potassium are the most common electrolytes in the human body. They're essential for many heart, nerve and muscle functions. They also play an important role in keeping fluid levels normal in different body compartments.

When imbalances occur in these electrolytes, whatever the causes may be, it can lead to medical issues linked with the nervous system, and the heart, in various degrees of severity. The body must maintain a balance between the water levels within the body and the electrolytes in order to function normally. The role of electrolytes is the maintain the delicate balance between water and all the various minerals and salts in the body. When this balance is out of balance due to a lack of electrolytes then one of the symptoms that can manifest in involuntarily muscles contractions and spasms.

Emotional states of Pluto transiting the 4th house *(5-HTP)*

(Q): The description of Pluto transiting through the fourth house doesn't sound like such a good time. The way you described the health problems of a person under this transit along with how the person can almost be catatonic as they absorb the shifting emotional states sounds like someone I know who is finishing this transit up. She is also a Cancer and has Pluto in Virgo conjunct the Moon and Uranus in Libra in the second. Do you recommend anything to benefit the afflicted areas of the body during this time?

(A): Anything that will create emotional stability and evenness, as the serotonin levels within the brain typically go haywire. A possibility is to supplement with a new compound called 5-HTP.

Emotional unrest

A great many of diseases are rooted in emotional unrest or emotional repression and this energy then manifesting in physical symptoms.

Epididymitis

(Q): I am currently counseling a client who suffers from

epididymitis (inflammation, pain and swelling in the structure which lies on and around each testicle). His birth data is August 13, 1971; 9:45 am; Vancouver, BC. I was thinking of pumpkin seeds and zinc, but would you recommend anything else?

(A): To my knowledge, that condition is caused by an external infection that is normally associated either with the person himself who is having intercourse with someone who is infected and/or a person who has a partner who is not being faithful: Contracting the infection from another and then giving it to their partner thru intercourse. The underlying source of the infection is normally treated with antibiotics. The remedies you mention can 'contain' it but not heal it.

Epilepsy

(Q1): Have you had clients with epilepsy: petite mal? I am assuming that it would be exacerbated with the Uranian transit through Aquarius and the new dendrite growth. Besides additional B-12 to support the myelinated nerves and Fo-ti tincture to support dendrite growth, are there other physical supplements you might recommend? This condition onset at puberty, not birth, following a head trauma, but there was no concussion.

(A): I don't know what else I would recommend.

(Q2): I had a client with epilepsy. She had a stellium in Libra in the first house, and I put her on Kava, which seemed to help. Another herbalist put her on Reishi Mushroom and a few other things that I could find out for you if you are interested.

(Q3): I suffer from seizures due to scar tissue from brain

tumor surgery 14 years ago. Interesting new studies on epilepsy in children show that going on a low carb diet for two years can eliminate seizures. Read Life Without Bread available from *www.lifeservices.com.* An endocrinologist explains it well.

Fats

Fats correlate to Saturn, Capricorn, and the 10th House because they are part of the natural structure of the body that promote healthy skin and hair, insulating body organs against shock, maintaining body temperature, and promoting healthy cell function. Fat also serves the function of storing energy within the body that it needs to use at all times: like money in the bank. Fat also serves as a vehicle to buffer the body against many types of disease by diluting from the bloodstream excessive levels of various substances that can cause disease.

This diluting process is then stored in the body by way of new fat substances that serve to insulate various body organs against these potential diseases until they can be eliminated by way of being metabolized or removed from the body via various forms of excretion.

Genetic imprinting, Soul intention

(Q): Can you explain the linkage between genetic/hereditary imprinting and what the Soul has specifically chosen astrologically? What I am having difficulty reconciling is the fact that we choose specific delineations in our birth chart and how that relates with the families we choose. In other words, are there some aspects and such that occur more randomly in accordance with more specific aspects we absolutely choose?

(A): Nothing is random at all in the birth chart. The whole chart correlates with the evolutionary and karmic intentions and necessities of any given Soul.

(B)(Q): Can we have hereditary linkage with one parent and karmic necessity with another?

(A): Anything in one's life correlates to one's evolutionary and karmic needs and intentions, including both parents. There is no such thing as 'just' hereditary linkage.

(Q): Would several septiles of a parent's planet to their child's north node, along with the child's Pluto conjunct this parent's north node indicate a situation where one is either coming in knowing they can rely on deep love, or that the child is somehow coming in to help that parent with their evolutionary necessity?

(A): Generally, that would be true.

(Q): Also, do you believe that any factor remains constant in the birth chart from one incarnation to the next (i.e., the degree on the ascendant)?

(A): Sometimes that happens, but it is not some absolute thing.

Herbs and dreams

(Q1): Is there an herb or combination of herbs that can be taken regularly to help stimulate whatever gland needs to be stimulated so that one may have more consistent dreams?

(A): Not to my knowledge.

(Q2): I work as an herbalist and know that people have dream experiences when they take Valerian. Personally, I don't get that from it, but try Gotu Kola. I have funky lucid dreams when I take it. In the herb's history, it was taken by medicine people to induce 'visions.' You don't need to overdo it, though; just take the suggested dosage on the back. It's very safe and good for many things!

Jupiter retrograde

(Q): You have said that Jupiter retrograde can correlate to problems with a person's metabolism due to a deficiency of iodine. Is there a natural treatment or remedy to improve that condition?

(A): Either natural kelp, which is full of iodine, or homeopathic iridium, which is iodine. Iridium is quite toxic, so if you choose to use that, visit a professional homeopath to determine the right dose for you.

Lupus

(Q): Can you suggest any herbs or supplements for a woman with lupus? Her most severe complaints are IBS, an inability to maintain potassium, and joint pain. Kidney test results are OK, but my feeling is there is a shutting down. Her father died with lupus due to kidney failure at 44; she is 48.

(A): I know of nothing to treat lupus. One thing that can help the joint pain is homeopathic calc phos and mag phos taken at a very high level. These two compounds induce the body to secrete synovial fluids, which are like lubricators for the joints and bones.

(Q): What primary indicators do you see for lupus in natal chart?

(A): Neptune receiving stressful aspects; planets in Pisces receiving stressful aspects; planets in the 12th house receiving stressful aspects; a stellium of Pisces planets in the sixth; Neptune in the fourth in opposition to Saturn, Uranus, or Pluto in the 10th; or Neptune squaring the nodes.

(Q): In this chart Pisces/Virgo are on the 12th/6th cusps, respectively, with no planets in either house; however, Neptune rx at 7 Libra is squared by Mars/Uranus/Moon in Cancer in the fourth.

(A): That's the genetic signature from her family of origin.

(Q): Her Sun/Mercury rx/Venus in Gemini in the third are inconjunct Saturn rx in Scorpio in the eighth.

(A): This now makes it specific to the father. To me, this is a pattern wherein the Soul did not want to be born into the current life in the first place relative to unresolved traumas from other times and carries a resistance to earth life because of this, which is the cause of the lupus.

Lymph system

(Q): What planet/sign rules the lymphatic system?

(A): Pluto and the Moon.

Manic depression

(Q): What are the astrological markers for manic depression?

(A): There are many markers, but it comes down to stressful dynamics between Saturn and Jupiter, or the rulers of one's 10th and fourth houses in a stressful aspect pattern, or the phasal relationship between Saturn and Jupiter being stressful, as in a full phase.

Medical correlations for a client

(Q): I have a client in 1st stage individuated with the following chart: The Ascendant is 14 Leo. Pluto is at 5 Virgo in the first house; the South Node is at 24 Pisces in the eighth house, conjunct Mercury at 16 Pisces in the eighth. Uranus is at 18 Leo in the first. Neptune and the Moon are conjunct at 9 and 15 Scorpio, respectively, in the fourth; Jupiter is at 28 Sagittarius in the fifth, and Saturn is at 14 Capricorn in the sixth. Mars/Venus are conjunct at 26/27 Capricorn in the sixth, and Chiron is at 27 Aquarius in the seventh conjunct a 29 degree Aquarian Sun. She is having pain in her pelvic area, lower back, hip, and upper thigh area on the right. She places it mostly in her root and sacral chakras, with 'spidery' energy extending up to the naval chakra. She says she feels like she's holding something from the past that now needs to be released, but she doesn't know what. With this signature, I'm thinking that there is blockage due to guilt from patriarchal conditioning concerning her sexuality, but I can't get beyond that and how to help her. I'd appreciate any help you could offer.

(A): This is a long and complicated situation involving deep conflicts between spirit and flesh and the guilt because of that. The underlying problem is the nature of the beliefs which serve as how she interprets phenomena: Jupiter square the nodes. As long as patriarchal beliefs are adhered to, then of course this conflict occurs. Because of this conflict, there have been many lives in which she has felt that she has 'sinned' against God because of the strong and dominant sexual energy that her Soul has carried. Within that, there is even a deep, repressed anger at the patriarchal God itself because of her sexual nature and identity.

I do not want to get into an extensive analysis, so let me say in short that because of this conflict leading to guilt, which, of course, she has needed to 'atone' for, she has created certain kinds of lives in which that atonement plays out in intense and severe ways. The last life would perfectly illustrate the situation. Her last life was during World War II in Japan, in which the government rounded up thousands of Japanese women to serve as sexual slaves for the Japanese army. She was then subjected to repeated sexual assaults of a sustained and ongoing basis resulting in an absolute loss of control, absolute humiliation and a deep sense of contamination because of this. This then correlates to memories within the Soul that manifest within the body as 'cellular memories,' and it is these memories that are causing the condition you speak of because the memories within the Soul are still deeply repressed due to the horrifying nature of them.

This repression thus affects the underlying 'circulation' of blood within her body, meaning it is restricted. In turn, this causes a buildup of 'lactic acid' in the red blood cells which in turn compounds and causes further restriction within the muscles and nerves, focusing in the lower back (Mars/Venus). This manifests as restriction upon the sciatic nerves, kidneys, and adrenals. It is this restriction on those nerves that causes the 'spidery' feeling that you speak of. This spidery effect is the nerves themselves relative to the electrical impulses.

The obvious Soul intention is to radically change her 'beliefs' in this life (Jupiter squaring nodes) from patriarchal to natural, which then changes how she not only interprets reality in general, but specifically reorienting to the natural and evolving God'ess. The resolution of the conflict between spirit and flesh resolves in this way. The remedies I would suggest she take would be 500 mg per day of pantothenic acid, which will dissolve the excessive build of the lactic acid, which will then allow the muscles and nerves to relax. Combine this with 200 mg per day of niacin to forcefully restore proper circulation, a complex B vitamin, and the Chinese herb Fo-ti taken as a tincture: 25 eye drops on the tongue three times per day. The specific remedy for the sciatic nerves is the herb wintergreen taken as a tea.

Physically, I would recommend hatha or raja yoga with specific emphasis on the 'spinal twist', the 'ear closing pose', and the cobra, which will serve as a fulcrum release for the energy build up and repression in the naval chakra. Prepare her for that one, because when she first does it, she will feel like she is doing a 360 in her head which is the symbol for the freeing up of the energy.

Medical situation doctors can't diagnose

(Q1): I have a client with a medical situation the doctors can't figure out. She has Mercury at 12 Sagittarius, the Sun at 15 Sagittarius, and an Ascendant of 18 Aquarius, with Pluto at 16 Leo on the Descendant. The transits have been tough for a while! They have monitored her and found that her heart beats regularly during the day but irregularly at night. She has been having mini strokes and has lost her sight in her left eye. Now her right eye is acting up. They don't know what it is but suspect it may be.

Melatonin

(Q): I woke up from a nap today in a space where I 'knew' what you mean when you say that melatonin dissolves the boundary between the egocentric consciousness and God. It raised a few questions. I've noticed I often tend to fall asleep with a light turned on. Even though my eyes are closed while I'm sleeping, does having a light on in the room affect the amount of melatonin produced?

(A): Yes.

(Q): I often either stay up most of the night, or else get up in the middle of the night, to write or to reflect. This is not insomnia. I find it much easier to access my true nature and feelings in the middle of the night. Is this related to melatonin production, even though I'm awake?

(A): Yes, because the melatonin has already been secreted while you were sleeping. Upon waking, especially when it is still dark out, there is a carry-over effect of this melatonin.

(Q): If it is related to melatonin, does being awake at night cause less melatonin to be produced than would be if I were asleep?

(A): Relatively, yes. But also remember that this hormone and protein is also relatively secreted even while awake, which is especially so for all Souls who are inherently creative by nature, inventive by nature, who are deeply inspired by nature, and so on. This is the actual physiology of those things.

(Q): Is there a long term detrimental effect if this is a regular pattern?

(A): No, because Souls who are inherently creative by nature don't sleep the socially conditioned way, which tells us we must have eight hours of sleep per night. In reality, the brain only needs four to five hours of sleep at most per day to totally renew. In fact, a recent study suggests that those folks who sleep less than eight hours (say 4 to 6 hours), actually live longer than those who sleep more than this. What this reflects is the strength of the underlying life force within such folks - very, very strong - and this tends to correlate to the creative, the artist, and inspired types among us. I also only sleep four to five hours a night, at most.

(Q): Also, is melatonin production affected by sunlight? In other words, if I nap during the day, is melatonin produced, since my eyes are closed, or does the fact that it's not night time limit melatonin production even though I'm sleeping in a dark room?

(A): It is still secreted, but not in the amounts produced while sleeping or dozing at night. For example, during the day time when we find ourselves 'spaced out,' this is an example of melatonin being produced even during the daytime.

Melatonin and spiritualizing process

(Q1): You mentioned in your tapes that light therapy suppresses the secretion of melatonin and, consequently, can be used to treat depression. Do increased levels of melatonin cause depression?

(A): Yes, it can. It can also be the causative factor in what is called manic-depression.

(B)(Q1): I'm a little confused because you also mentioned that melatonin acts to dissolve the boundaries separating the subjective egocentric consciousness from Soul consciousness. In essence, melatonin acts as a spiritualizing process. How does melatonin connect with depression and act as a spiritualizing agent at the same time?

(A): When one consciously begins the journey to truly spiritualize, melatonin is increased within the brain/consciousness in order to dissolve the apparent boundary between the current ego and the Soul. As this occurs, the Soul then becomes increasingly aware, consciously, of the Source of All Things: actual inner 'cosmic' consciousness in varying degrees of realization - the Ultimate, the Absolute. As a result of this, when the consciousness is then 'snapped' back to 'normal' reality - life on earth with all that that means and implies - the contrast that one's consciousness is then presented with causes, for many, a transiting state of depression. This depression is caused by the inner knowledge that one must complete whatever the current life is about - the gravity of time and space, mortality, the baggage of the 'body,' the baggage of the totality of what the life is about.

(Q1): Also, is it correct to say that if you are not tuned into this spiritualizing process the melatonin can in some people become "misdirected" and become a causal factor in psychic disturbances?

(A): Yes, it can be a causative factor in all kinds of neuroses and psychoses.

(Q2): As one moves into the spiritual state, would it be of great importance, because of this "snap back" you mentioned, to not only be very aware of this effect of melatonin on the conscious being, but also to be able to manage the melatonin so as to not get unbalanced?

(A): Melatonin is naturally regulated by the entire brain. When one is supplementing with melatonin then, yes, one must be careful.

Migraines

In my opinion these are caused, anatomically and

physiologically speaking, first by compressed adrenal glands, caused by excessive stress on one kind or the other, that then causes a great imbalance of the adrenaline and cortisone that is secreted by them. In turn this infuses the blood stream which then causes compression within the medulla area of the brain that then affects the chemical messages emanating from the hypothalamus that is regulating all the instinctual functions of the body. This will then cause the fatty linings within the nervous system to progressively break down that then impacts on how the electrical wiring, dendrites, synapses, neurons, receptor cells, etc., function. In turn this then affects the neurotransmitters that, when all of this is combined, create migraine headaches.

I have found working with such clients that the first order of business to heal this is to restore proper circulation of the blood system, the cardiovascular system, which starts by re-balancing the adrenal glands. Thus, good natural remedies that will do this start with pantothenic acid, niacin, a quality complex b vitamin, and magnesium. Hot bath infused with Epsom salts, a deep tissue massage as in Swedish type massages, and very deep regulated breathing over a period of time will all help.

(Q): I have a client who has been suffering from migraines since she was 12, and they are now exacerbated by menopause. Is there a particular signature in the chart for migraines, and do you have some suggestions for natural methods to alleviate them? Also, was it licorice root that you recommend during menopause?

(A): Typically, Uranus is implicated thru stressful aspects, or a stacked 11th house, or a bunch of planets in Aquarius. She can use a combination of pantothenic acid, niacin, B complex, and an herbal tincture of Fo-ti. Frequent deep tissue massage and frequent hot baths full of Epsom salts will also help. Yes to the licorice root, and also catnip herb.

Multiple Sclerosis

(Q): I take it that Saturn in Aquarius, or in stressful aspect to Uranus, could indicate possible MS. Since medical research also points to it being an autoimmune disorder that affects the central nervous system, could we also look to stressful aspects between Neptune and Uranus, Uranus in Pisces, etc.? Could we also pull in Mercury as the lower octave of Uranus? What else might be an indicator?

(A): Mars in stressful aspect to Uranus or Neptune; Uranus or Neptune in the third house with stressful aspects to them; Uranus or Neptune in the sixth or 12th house with stressful aspects to them.

I have Carl Jansky's book and Eileen Nauman's, but are there any other good reference books in print? In looking at Eileen Nauman's book I found reference to orotic acid as ruled by Pluto and which regenerates cells. "MS is thought to stem from a deficiency of orotic acid." This is also called Vitamin B-13. Have you heard of it? Uranus in Aquarius is also related to nerve degeneration, blurring of vision and strokes. The doctors are at a loss and say she's "going fast." Do you know of anything that can help her?

(Q2): Reinhold Ebertin's "Astrological Healing: The History and Practice of Astromedicine" is still in print and available through amazon.com.

I still have so much to learn about the medical stuff. Is your client's Mercury Sun in the 10th or 11th house? You mention that Uranus in Aquarius relates to nerve degeneration, blindness and strokes; i.e., if the Sun is in the 11th, this could relate to the blindness in the left eye (woman), and also to the strokes. But then what are the causes of/reasons for this? Is her Moon in Pisces or Aquarius? I'll be interested to see the answer about this as well.

(A): I would have to see the whole chart. There is not enough information in what you have presented. One compound that may help would be lipoic acid, which acts as a precursor to boost all natural physiological functions of the body.

It is also the number one remover of free radicals and acts to reverse degenerating nerves wherever they may exist in the body. The correct dosage would be 200 mg per day combined with magnesium and calcium.

(Q1): Her birth data is December 7, 1948; 11:33 am; Oklahoma City, OK. Her Sun/Mercury conjunction is in the tenth squaring her eight degree Pisces Moon in the first and eight degree Virgo Saturn in the seventh. She runs a hypnotherapy institute and runs herself ragged (Capricorn Mars conjunct Jupiter in the 11th). Thanks for the lipoic acid suggestion. If you see any more, it would really be appreciated.

Natural antidepressants

(Q): Is there any herbal remedy you can or would recommend as a natural antidepressant for those suffering from deep and frequent debilitating depressions (as reflected in harsh natal Saturn aspects, and/or heavy natal Capricorn/Virgo energy)?

(A) Yes, the herb damiana or the herb valerian. Homeopathically, try pulsatilla or ignatia.

Neptunian Instabilities

(Q): Are there indicators in the chart, either natal or progressions, that would indicate specific time frames for the potential of manic and/or psychotic breaks? This person, male, is saddled with Parkinson's disease, is taking dopamine and other drugs to control it and occasionally suffers from extreme paranoid delusions/ hallucinations. (He was in the Marines Special Forces division in Vietnam). The episodes can get rather intense, raising concerns for the safety of family members. This may be a side effect of occasional drug prescription mismanagement on the part of the individual, for a past history exists of extensive recreational drug usage. He has a natal Moon conjunct Neptune in Virgo in the seventh house; Uranus conjuncts the retrograde south node in Taurus in the third; Venus in Leo squares the nodes and trines Saturn in Aries in the second; Uranus trines Neptune; Pluto conjuncts Mercury in Cancer in the fifth; Jupiter in Pisces in the 12th is on the ascendant.

He appears to be seeking connection to the source or higher truths only in others and deeply fears or cannot access alone the place where his inner connection lies. Is this reflective of the south node conjunct Uranus, some past life fears relative to his individuation? If so, is this further compounded by the Moon/Neptune conjunction in seventh, putting him in situations that challenge his internal security to self-actualize/individuate? In your tapes, you indicated that the seventh and 12th houses can correlate to various forms of mental instabilities. Is this such a signature? One other question, when a seventh house Moon conjunct Neptune looks continually to others for their connection to the Source, is it accurate to say that what they need to be guided to do is find it within oneself through their first house signature?

(A): The person you have asked about comes to this life with what a psychologist would call 'hysteria dysplasia,' which is unresolved hysteria linked with unresolved traumas in recent lives. In relation to the Moon/Neptune/ seventh/Virgo/ Pisces/Jupiter, Uranus/south node conjunction, Venus squaring the nodes/Uranus, this is essentially a Soul who has created recent lifetimes in which massive loss of life was occurring relative to political/religious wars, including the loss of his own family, and his own life.

This is the basis of the unresolved trauma/hysteria, which then creates a dynamic within him of never feeling safe anywhere, feeling like 'something' can always happen. When mental instability is indicated natally, Neptune, Uranus, the 11th house, Aquarius, Pisces, and/or the 12th house will always be indicated in some fashion. The transits of these planets can correlate to 'timing' of when the underlying signature of mental instability becomes more active than at others.

Nose

The nose is partially Uranus because it is responsible for taking in Oxygen. It is part of the entire structure that takes in oxygen in the body. From this perspective even the mouth could have a correlation to Uranus.

Osteoporosis

(Q): You have mentioned licorice root as being helpful for osteoporosis. Do you have a special blend, and if so, is it still possible to get this?

(A): No, I have no special blend; it is just the use of the herb by itself.

The body ♄, ♏, 10·H.

MEDICAL ASTROLOGY

Pain

The nature of pain is to inform the brain to take action relative to what the specific type of pain is in order to take necessary remedial action before a cataclysmic situation is reached.

Panic/anxiety attacks

(Q): What planets and signs correlate to the psychological phenomenon of panic attacks, or anxiety attacks? Perhaps it is a Mercury-Neptune or 12th house correlation?

(A): Yes, that combination could correlate to 'panic attacks,' relative to what is called hysteria dysplasia or unresolved trauma from the past that has become emotionally displaced. In general, anxiety attacks are a function of unresolved trauma in one form or another. Thus, in general, Uranus, the 11th House, and Aquarius have this correlation. The lower octave of Uranus is Mercury, so the behavioral manifestation of such things can manifest thru Mercury, Gemini, or Virgo, but this planet and these signs are not the causative factors.

Physical body, rulership of

(Q): Do Aries/Mars/1st House correlate to the physical body? If not, what does?

(A): No, it does not. The various signs, planets, and houses all correlate to different parts of the body and its physiology. The body in total, as a 'container' for the Soul, correlates to Saturn, Capricorn, and the 10th house.

Plutonian repression (constipation) in relation to Pluto transits

(Q): Is there a remedy, ritual or technique you recommend to relieve periods of deeply compressed constipation. This is only for certain periods of severe constipation brought on by a Plutonian transit, when the famous Plutonian repression even outpowers the lifelong remedy of Sanicle tincture. Is there a method to physically induce the Plutonian person into coming into direct contact with the repression? Any sort of ritual that will help unblock and free the Plutonian person at such a deeply repressed time or help them uncover why is this happening at this particular period?

(A): Yes, if the degree of compressed constipation is such that not even the sanicle tincture works, then a much more intense method needs to be employed: self-administered colonics. You will find in so doing that even the act of drawing water into yourself, when it begins to reach the upper recesses, will in fact produce quite a bit of pain until the compressed material is removed. Even the act of eliminating the water from within will usually generate a lot of 'heat' and physical discomfort. It is exactly when this heat or pain occurs that you can feel deeply within what this discomfort and heat is linked to: actual cellular memories. So if you have the courage to look at it, you can probably find out what the cause of all this is. Normally, it is linked with unresolved trauma of a sexual or emotional nature.

Pluto transit, health problems

(Q): What are the health problems that could occur when transiting Pluto opposes natal Saturn and squares the natal Moon at the same time? Is it a sure thing that the person will endure continual depression, or is there a way to avoid continuous depression during a transit like this?

(A): A lot would depend on the actual houses of the natal Saturn and Moon. In general, on a medical level it can correlate to a buildup of toxins within the bone marrow, which is then reflected through the lymphatic and endocrine systems. The first symptom for that is swelling and a breakdown in the integrity of the b and t cells that manifest from the bone marrow, which can then implicate immune system issues. There can be a loss of relevant levels of calcium, magnesium, phosphorus, iron, and iodine relative to the thyroid, as well as an imbalance between the white and red blood cells, with the worst case manifesting as leukemia. An imbalance in the digestive enzymes can cause digestive problems and an imbalance in insulin can indicate pancreatic problems. There can be eruptions on the skin: boils, tumors, and abscesses, as well as a buildup of water behind the eye, as in glaucoma.

In a woman's chart, there can be problems in the uterus and/or ovaries, vaginal infections, strange discharges through the vagina, with the worst case manifesting as uterine, ovarian, or cervical cancer or fibroid type tumors within the womb or cysts on the ovaries.

These are examples of what can happen, but it is not an exhaustive list. Psychologically, the intent is reflection upon the past, with this reflection manifesting typically as what folks call depression, but depression again is really reflection. The intent in this reflection is to focus on all the existing inner dynamics that have been in place in such a way as to determine how each dynamic has been responsible for creating the person's life circumstances to date. The intent within this is to learn in hindsight and then to apply what is learned to the new evolutionary cycle that is trying to be born so that the past is not duplicated into the future. In addition, this transit can correlate to an almost total loss of meaning for living, no sense of real purpose anymore. The worst case scenarios can produce thoughts of suicide or actual suicide. The consequence to a person who has no sense of purpose or meaning for living is, of course, suicide. Intense emotions like grief, self-defeat, and futility can all manifest for no 'apparent' reason.

Root of any ailment

EA is able to determine the 'why" of just about anything. Thus, specific symptoms all have their own causes. EA is able to determine, in almost all cases, the cause of anything. Each case, Soul, is unique. This is why it is essential to have a firm grasp and understanding of the core principles, methodology, of EA so that the why or cause of whatever condition can be understood. So to understand the root of any ailment it is essential to understand EA itself. This very thread on medical astrology will hopefully help all of us towards this end.

Saturn and bad back

(Q): I know someone who has a disc that slipped out a few years ago and now is experiencing stomach problems. Chiropractors have not been able to help her pop the disc in but only to relieve the pain for a short while. In her chart she has Saturn in the 10th house in Gemini opposing Jupiter in Scorpio and Neptune in Sagittarius in the fourth, with all this squaring the nodes, which are the south node in Leo in the 12th and the north node conjunct Mars in Aquarius in the sixth. Is this the reliving of some old trauma, and/or do these symbols indicate that it is a "chronic" condition that must be experienced for some reason? Also transiting Uranus is currently passing over the north node/Mars.

(A): Yes, this is a karmic pattern, which means it was fated from birth. The cause is unresolved traumas of a sexual and psychological nature that are deeply repressed relative to the naval and root chakras, thus the conditions that you describe. Also, the entire sciatic nervous system would be implicated, which will compound the problem, along with the pancreas, duodenum, and liver with sympathetic reactions in the colon and intestine and the peristaltic action therein. The current transit you point out means it is time for her to address those suppressed traumas and the reasons she needed to create them for herself - to own them versus being a victim to them - then the karma will be removed and the conditions will stabilize.

(Q): As she confronts these issues and begins to deal with them are there any foods/herbs that would help ease the symptoms and/or things that should be avoided so as not to irritate the different organs/nervous system/spine?

(A): A tincture of sanicle, 25 eye drops per day; the herb wintergreen, made into a tea; colonics that have a pinch of the herb catnip, which helps promote tonality and peristaltic action; 500 mg per day of pantothenic acid; vitamin B complex; and niacin. She should build up her system slowly with the niacin; perhaps use 25mg of the 'flush' kind at a time, and work up to about 300 mg per day. She can also use Vitalitea and do some yoga postures like the cobra for sure, and the spinal twist. And she should get deep tissue massage.

Saturn correlations

(Q): In my somewhat limited notes from class last year I have the following correlations for Saturn and am just checking on accuracy: B & T cells, skeleton, marrow (source of B&T cells), spinal discs, structure of brain, skin, key minerals in body, manic depression, migraines.

I also recorded that Pluto is the ruler of the spine. Since the spine is part of the skeleton, is Pluto like a sub ruler within the skeletal system of the area of the spine? If so, are there other sub rulers of the skeleton, like the skull (Aries, Mars), the hands (Gemini/Mercury), but all under the primary rulership of Saturn (bones)?

(A): Pluto correlates to the 'sushumna' of the actual fluids within the spinal column. Yes, to the sub rulers.

Sensing – Venus and Neptune

These planets, the signs the rule, and the houses they correlate too sensing as a general physiological and anatomical response to the inner and outer environments that provide essential information to the brain. Why ? Because astrology is a natural science which means a science of correlation and observation versus theory or hypothesis. Thus, through direct observation and correlations over a great length of time of the human being these correlations to these planets, etc., have been observed.

Spinal disc damage

(Q): My son's stepdaughter is currently in Germany in the Army. The doctor is going to run an MRI on her, as he suspects disc damage. Considering that she has Saturn in Scorpio in the third in a new phase conjunction to Pluto in Libra in the third, this is probably genetic damage. The Saturn/Pluto conjunction opposes her Aries Sun and Mars in Taurus in the ninth and inconjuncts her Venus in Gemini in the 10th. What would be the holistic approach to help the problem?

(A): To help her understand the psychological causes for the physical condition. This signature also correlates to a high degree of stress in the adrenals, kidneys, and sciatic nerves.

Stabilizing the brain

(Q): I have a client with the following: south node combust Mercury in Taurus in the ninth house and conjunct Jupiter in Taurus in the ninth, all in opposition to a Uranus/south node conjunction in Scorpio in the third. Uranus and Jupiter both square Saturn in Cancer in the 12th, trine a Scorpio Moon in the fourth (Scorpio Moon rules the 12th) in loose balsamic conjunction to Neptune in Sagittarius in the fourth, with Neptune forming a sesquiquadrate to the Saturn. Mars is in Cancer in the 11th and is balsamic to Saturn and inconjunct Neptune in the fourth and trine the Uranus/north node. Would this be a case where the 5-HTP you talked about at Astro 2000 could be used to stabilize the brain?

(A): Yes, certainly 5-HTP, but also homeopathic ignatia and pulsatilla and a tincture of Fo-ti.

Stress – flight or fight

Hormones, in general, correlate with Scorpio, Pluto, and the 8th House. Venus correlates as a co-ruler with Pluto to cortisol. The adrenals also secrete the hormones Epinephrine (adrenaline) which correlates to Mars with the co-ruler Pluto and Norepinephrine which correlate with Saturn and Pluto. Thus the 'flight or fight' as you put it. Stress, whatever the causes may be, disrupts the equilibrium, balance, between these hormones. Thus, in the signature that we are looking into, Mars in opposition to Uranus, stress then can cause extreme imbalances of these hormones relate to the adrenals. This then creates a high degree of adrenal stress that can lead to adrenal fatigue, or outright collapse of the adrenals. When that takes place a variety of other medical conditions can then take place.

Stress moves in a perpetual feedback loop affecting all levels experienced, ie physically, emotionally, psychologically, spiritually.

Suffering

Suffering in the context of 'why' any given Soul has created the conditions for its life so that all Souls can take responsibility for that which, in fact, they have created for themselves. Understanding the causes, the why's of anything, equals self-knowledge. When this is then known to a Soul it is then up to them to do what is necessary to make the changes that can lead them in new evolutionary directions that can hopefully eliminate the conditions that have created whatever types of pain they have. Of course many Souls have created conditions in which the pain they have, the nature of it, cannot be alleviated at all and/or can only be modified to some extent. The reasons for this, the why, is unique to each Soul. EA can help uncover whatever those unique reasons are for any given Soul.

Sweat

Sweat is a water that is filled with various minerals that the body via the sympathetic nervous system activates in order to regulate the body's temperature. Because of the connection to the sympathetic nervous system there is a correlation to Uranus. Additionally, the body temperature is regulated by the heart rate, and thus the Sun. It is not an electrolyte. There are sweat electrolyte tests that are aimed at determining the levels of chloride within the sweat. But, of itself, sweat is not an electrolyte. Because sweat is a water its primary correlation with the natural trinity of the 4th, 12th, and 8th houses, Cancer, Pisces, Scorpio, and Pluto, Neptune, and the Moon. To me the lead in this is the 4th house, Cancer, and the Moon which then has as its natural polarity Saturn, Capricorn, and the 10th house that then correlates to the various minerals within the sweat. The sweat gland itself correlates with Pluto, Scorpio, and the 8th house.

Trauma and Aquarius

(Q)In the first Measuring the Night, there is discussion regarding trauma in the birth chart. If Aquarius is figured prominently in the symbolism of Pluto and/or the south node of the Moon or its ruler, does this always indicate trauma?

(A): No. Aquarius, Uranus, and the 11th house is a total archetype like any other sign/planet/house, and one of the dimensions within that totality of that archetype is the dynamic of trauma.

(Q): Is it always related to from breaking away from the dictates of society if Saturn is involved in the symbolism?

(A): No, there can be a variety of possible astrological signatures that can correlate to that.

(Q): In trying to integrate the archetype of Aquarius with the idea of trauma, does it always mean the root cause of the trauma is to cause detachment and awareness of the rooted behaviors found through further evaluation of the symbols?

(A): It depends on the nature and severity of the trauma itself. Depending on the severity it can, and in many cases does, equal an initial 'fragmentation' within the Soul/personality. It is like a bomb going off that creates the initial destruction and then sends whatever was exploded into the air in all kinds of pieces. Then the pieces begin to fall back to the ground, but they are now totally rearranged from the original form that was exploded.

A fundamental alteration with the structure of the Soul occurs because of the trauma, the shock to it. This creates the post-traumatic stress disorder dynamic wherein certain environmental 'triggers' can cause behaviors that are 'irrational' relative to the environmental stimulus. The effects can be very long lasting, which means these effects can last lifetimes.

(Q): Another issue with the archetype, for some of these individuals, is the idea of reliance on the group, fitting in. Does the fear of individuality come from the trauma, and therefore anonymity is desired in subsequent lifetimes?

(A): For some the process of 'individuating', moving beyond the consensus, has caused, for their own reasons, trauma from the environment relative to the judgments of the consensus. The are many possibilities for traumas of this kind. An example would be intense persecutions from the consensus that were so severe that the reaction to that could cause the individual to want to 'hide' from that consensus by way of trying to look and be like everyone else.

Trauma signature

(Q): I want to understand the signature for trauma more fully. I read your article, 'Trauma and the Outer Planets'. Even if

the outer planets have stressful aspects, the individual is not necessarily under the trauma influence. Is that correct?

(A): Right.

(Q): Does it mean, though, that the person experienced a traumatic situation in a past life that may or may not have been repressed or suppressed?

(A): Very commonly, when you see stressful aspects to the planets that correlate with trauma, it does correlate to trauma. The stressful aspects tend to correlate to traumas that have been so severe that they have not been dealt with. The non-stressful aspects tend to correlate to traumas that have been dealt with.

(Q): Is it possible that a person suffers from trauma, but externally in their behavior it is still very hard to detect?

(A): Yes. Typically, the main give away is 'stunted speech,' or behavioral reactions to an existing stimulus that manifest as behavior that is disproportionate the stimulus itself.

(Q): Basically, at what point do you say whether a person requires therapy for suppressed trauma? (perhaps because of obvious external behavioral patterns).

(A): When a person becomes essentially dysfunctional and unable to integrate into daily living in such a way as to carry on a 'normal' life.

Trauma, past lives and planetary nodes

(Q): I have a question about planetary nodes –

Aquarius/Neptune/Uranus/Pisces/Libra/Capricorn, 10th, 11th, and 12th houses and trauma. What type of trauma would be indicated if the south node of Neptune is conjunct Venus, Mercury, and Jupiter in Aquarius intercepted in the 10th and also widely conjunct the MC at 29 Capricorn 57 (Capricorn also on ninth)? The north node of both Venus and Neptune conjunct Pluto retrograde intercepted in Leo in the fourth; the north nodes of both Saturn and Jupiter conjunct the IC; and Saturn is retrograde in Virgo in the fifth. Pisces is on the 11th and natal Neptune retrograde in Libra in the sixth is conjunct the south node in the fifth, along with Mars retrograde (north node rule) in Libra. The Moon is in Taurus in the 12th; Sun in Pisces in the 10th; south node of Uranus is conjunct Chiron in Sagittarius in the eighth; and Uranus is retrograde in Cancer in the second, squaring the nodal axis. What if the north and south nodes of Pluto and Saturn fall into Capricorn in the ninth, but the south node of Jupiter is not in Capricorn; it's at 29 Sagittarius 02 minutes in the eighth conjunct Chiron?

I can see the accepting responsibility for your own reality part, and trauma linked to disillusionment, mental, emotional, physical/sexual, psychic and spiritual trauma. There's a lot of parallel symbolism in the 'martyr' example in the book, with some radical contras. I would like to run past you what I've come up with. This Soul was also persecuted and put to death for her beliefs and her message. Unlike the Soul in the example, it caused her to suppress her true self, and to mistrust herself and others. She essentially became detached from her Soul. She also may have allowed herself to be intimidated into delivering a system message/action in which she did not believe, and has much guilt as a result. In this lifetime she is to come out and publicly deliver a message, but change the way she has delivered it in the past so as not to threaten people or endanger herself.

She is to regain her courage, self-worth and inner calm, (integrate body, mind and spirit) and become more self-reliant and have a sense of personal authority to successfully integrate into the existing system without selling out, or losing sight of, her individuality or purpose. She is also to become more discerning about who and what she sacrifices for. With Pallas in Scorpio in the sixth, she may have worked behind the scenes or underground for a cause. With Hildago conjunct the Libra south node configuration, freedom, equality, and justice are important to her, perhaps having fought for those in the past. With Chiron in the eighth conjunct the south nodes of both Uranus and Jupiter, she will attempt to allow these old wounds to die, and be reborn in Aries north node in the 11th. Active spirituality will be an important part of this 'rebirth'. She will have a lot of emotional/ psychological baggage to work through to accomplish this, some of this dealing with her present life mother.

I would really like to understand this past life trauma stuff a lot better because I'm convinced it affects us all much more than most would believe. What is hysteria dysplasia? I've been unable to find that term any place I've looked.

(A): Yes, your analysis of those symbols is pretty much right on. You left out some of what correlates to unresolved trauma - specifically sexual trauma - and hysteria dysplasia, which is simply emotional hysteria caused by severe trauma that remains unresolved, thus displaced. Typically, hysteria dysplasia will also cause multiple personalities disorder, or now what is called 'dissociative behavior.'

Uranus transiting Pisces

(Q): I find myself grappling with the archetype of Pisces and

Neptune. Does the transit of Uranus in Pisces across angular houses have a greater impact on an individual's chart?

(A): Yes.

(Q): And if this transit is aspecting a natal chart with planets in Pisces, what kind of energy is it generating?

(A): To liberate from any existing dynamics that are preventing maximum individual actualization relative to one's true nature.

(Q): Personally, for me this transit feels so very significant. I have Pisces at five degrees on my MC, with Saturn retrograde conjunct Chiron which opposes Pluto conjunct Uranus in my fourth house. Physically, what do I need to be watchful of and what herbs and/or supplements can I take to assist me during this stressful transit?

(A): Digestive issues caused thru the pancreas; skin conditions due to the body trying to purge existing toxins; a dehydration of synovial fluids, which can cause aching in the joints; a deficiency in calcium, magnesium, and phosphorus; lymph gland swelling, again due to toxins trying to come out; potential disruptions in the balance of the white and red blood cells; deficiency in iron; spontaneous kundalini secretions throughout the body producing symptoms which can include feeling numbness in various areas of the body and/or sometimes a kind of paralysis in different areas of the body; alternating between feeling very hot to feeling very cold; tingling sensations in various areas of the body; migraines; intense pressure in the back of the neck/skull, which is a reflection of the hypothalamus, and so on.

Herbs: sanicle as a tincture, Fo-ti as a tincture, the upplements for the lack of different minerals as above, frequent deep tissue massage, frequent hot baths with Epsom salts, niacin, vitamin B-complex, and pantothenic acid, lipoic acid, and frequent 'sun baths.'

5 PRACTICE CHARTS

STEP 1

Examine the correlations that have been provided about the anatomy, physiology, and the chakra systems and then link those correlations to the example: Mars opposed Uranus. So, in this example we would simply refer to the correlations of Mars, Aries, and the 1st house to the correlations of Uranus, Aquarius, and the 11th house and put that in the context of an opposition. There is no need to read medical books.

CHART A – Potential medical issues of Mars inopposition to Uranus in a male body

Practice Charts by

- Katherine
- Skywalker
- Kristin
- Ari Moshe
- Linda
- Gonzalo
- Upasika

CHART A – Potential medical issues of Mars in opposition to Uranus in a male body

Practice Chart by Katherine

I'm guessing that this would be a volatile signature (I

visualized a strap fight. A strap fight involves two people who are bound together by a length of rope, chain, or a belt. Forced engagement - with zero chance of escape - is the objective. Forced opposition - a dynamic stasis) with both Uranus and Mars relating to Yang and Pranic energies engaged through a cardinal association.

Both symbols, archetypically, have a stressful/caustic nature, manifesting the instincts for separation and freedom in different ways. Visually, I think it's an interesting tension with Uranus correlating to Kundalini/root chakra energy concurrently with trauma, disassociation, and vacating. Mars registers to the navel/solar plexus chakra, conversely, linking to violence, sex, and procreation. (I visualized a lemniscate.)

Air*Uranus (fire*opposition) Fire*Mars as experienced by the human body, to me, would indicate the long-term situation of nervous system burnout via exhaustion (flame continuously stoked). Stress moves in a perpetual feedback loop affecting all levels experienced ie physically, emotionally, psychologically, and spiritually? Chronic stress flattens into fatigue, which can lead to frustration, and then anger. This lack of perspective tends to project upon others creating defensiveness and hyper-vigilance, possibly attracting antagonistic, hostile, or violent situations. Further, REM sleep is disturbed, compounding all experiences.

Constant, unrelenting stress could indicate Chronic Fatigue Syndrome. I think of PTSD as event/environmentally oriented—it has a definite beginning. So to me this would come through following a traumatic event in the present life (via transit/ progression) or, if from events in a previous life (indicated by the position of Pluto/S.Node) I think it is certainly a possibility but, looking at the difference, I am favoring CFS because of the broad scope and that the etiology (origin/causation) is unclear. ('When no etiology can be ascertained, the disorder is said to be idiopathic' ie 'arising spontaneously or from an obscure or unknown cause.') Also, PTSD tends to be a catchall for stress disorders that have manifested into human behavior. Similar to how fibromyalgia is diagnosed in cases where symptoms don't paint a clear picture or the causes are unclear.

Potential for other bursting-Uranus, fast, intense, and painful-Mars/Pluto cataclysmic experiences such as aneurism, heart attack, pulmonary embolism, etc. (From recent experiences I think these events are born not from a simple birth signature, but a perfect storm of natal, transit, progression and also environmental context/lifestyle owing much to level of consciousness, self-awareness, and self-care.)

Another possibility, looking at the anatomical and physiological attributes of each, could create the event of a stroke. Caused by ischemia - leaning toward Uranus caused by hemorrhage - leaning toward Mars. (I've just seen epilepsy in a natal chart as a Uranus-Mars crescent square and, a seizure by way of a Mars transit: opposing natal Mars, squaring natal Uranus—among other things.)

In a male form there could be a challenge to integrate oscillating extremes with regard to sexual desire fueled by intense endocrine rhythms, eg testosterone/adrenaline. Objectification, vacating, withdrawal (Uranus) then the acute need to act on primal, imperative, desires (Mars). (Perhaps other signatures could flavor this Experience, ie Saturn-guilt/shame, Jupiter – justification/glamour?) I just have a general sense of a drive to engage physically but, an inconsistency (lack/abundance, up/down) of energy to deliver.

Correlations –

Blood/Veins/Arteries: I looked into the conductivity of blood to see if there was a link to alkalinity. Conductivity increases as ionic (TDS) presence increases. A basic case for hydration! Varicosity, Varicocele Breath/Lungs/Trachea: as CO2 increases, acidity increases which, lead to a host of physical maladies (Bohr effect), eg acidosis, hyperviscosity, and hypercoagulability → thrombophilia, thrombosis (clot) (O2 intake effects pH more than diet) dry/dehydrated, asthma, hyperventilation GI/Duodenum / Esophagus-Mars dry / dehydrated, easily irritated, acid reflux, ulcers, Crohn's Endocrine: Imbalances of adrenaline, testosterone, cortisol (Cushing's), and acetylcholine (Alzheimer's) all can interfere with REM sleep, DHEA, androgen (a strong Pluto or Neptune aspect might pull this into a condition of intersex). Sex/Sex organs: dynamic libido, appear virile though may have imbalances that prevent 'performance.' Compromised sperm count, oligozoospermia.

Remedial efforts: Serious avoidance of stimulants, alcohol, excitotoxins, and neurotoxins, consistent REM sleep, pure water, calming smells - sage, alkalizing foods, herbs, mucilages and flavonoids. Since the Uranus-Mars opposition is so dynamic (and potentially combative) routine pranayama and asana. Sitting in a position that opens and grounds the root chakra (perineum/CV1). Breathing with eyes closed (quieting/non-threatening sensory deprivation) that is full and engages the diaphragm, massaging the viscera (Anapanasati - observing the sensation of the breath (Uranus) through the nostrils - balancing the nadis (left-inertia; right-action). This opening of the lungs aides 'CO2 disposal, preventing ammonia, ketones and aromatic amines from building up to toxic levels.' Increases circulation without exertion. Asanas that put the pelvis in line or above the heart and brain without exertion such as uttanasana, virasana, prasarita padottanasana, and savasana.

CHART A – Potential medical issues of Mars in opposition to Uranus in a male body

Practice Chart by Skywalker

Energetic imbalance between middle layer of Root chakra corresponding to one's individuating function, and the Navel chakra which corresponds to one's personal will power. The imbalance is shown by the opposition aspect and will correlate to stress between these two dynamics. As Mars is instinctive and Uranus unpredictable, this is a very volatile person who can become angry/irritable in a split second, with no apparent warning and with the potential for an uncontrollable temper. This can lead to high levels of psychological, emotional and physical stress. Stress as we know can cause all sorts of medical conditions and diseases.

Some potential conditions that can manifest with this planetary combination are: High levels of adrenaline as a result of stress, effecting heart rate. Heart attack due to the contracting of the arteries and muscle tissues and/or thickening of the blood. Aneurism due to the bursting of a vein in the brain. Pulmonary embolism due to clotting of the blood. Varicose veins due to dehydration. Over sensitized nervous system which can lead to shaking, over sensitivity to pain and electricity or other stimulus including sexual stimulus which leads to over excitement and pre-mature ejaculation, tense muscles that contract and don't let blood flow properly to them, muscular spasms, headaches and a highly nervous and reactive individual all round.

Other potential conditions:

- Irregular breathing which can lead to fatigue due to lack of oxygen.
- Possible brain damage from birth.
- Erratic physical movements.
- Hormonal imbalances in the adrenal glands due to irregular sexual desires, stress, anger, anxiety, which can lead to peaks/bursts of energy or a lack of energy and fatigue.
- Hormonal imbalances in the hypothalamus which can effect testosterone production and metabolic rate, leading to chronic fatigue amongst other conditions.

CHART A – Potential medical issues of Mars in opposition to Uranus in a male body

Practice Chart by Kristin

I realize the list of possibilities is long with this signature and it is also relative depending on the Soul's choices (Mars), stage of evolution as well as other signatures in the chart but here are some potential possibilities.

This Soul would not have most likely come into this life with unresolved trauma. Trauma is linked with Uranus and the opposition to Mars reflects being born with some form of PTSD. There may be events that would have created potentially more trauma, resulting in THE INABILITY TO EVER REALLY RELAX for they may always be wondering or worrying when the next shoe will drop because of experiencing prior unexpected traumas that may have caught them by surprise. The accumulated stress over time also due to the PTSD would cause the whole system to be in a constant state of tension. This kind of pressure and tension would increase the stress on the heart and the entire blood (Mars) stream, causing potential for heart attack or in extreme cases a brain aneurysm which occurs where there is a weak area in the wall of an artery that supplies blood to the brain causing a stroke. "The most common location for brain aneurysms is in the network of blood vessels at the base of the brain called the circle of Willis."

The elevated stress on the body due to an over active nervous system can affect all of the organs over time, especially the heart organ and the blood vessels as they as a result will have to be working harder to keep up with the pace of the potential higher blood pressure and heart rate that can accompany PTSD. A red blood cells (Mars) main function is carrying oxygen in the blood to various cells in the body, it uses a protein called hemoglobin for that purpose, where it picks up oxygen (Uranus) in the lungs and distributes it to the cells in the rest of the body.

A stroke is a condition in which the brain cells suddenly die because of a lack of oxygen. This can be caused by an obstruction in the blood flow, or the rupture of an artery that feeds the brain. The patient may suddenly lose the ability to speak, there may be memory problems, or one side of the body can become paralyzed.

This Soul will has the potential for sudden HEAD (Mars) injuries of a traumatic kind though some kind of unforeseen accident that could impact the spinal cord (Uranus). The opposition reflects the potential severity of a potential injury, that will range depending on other factors in the chart from moderate to severe as in paralysis. You can see this in a hard blow to the head in a football game, a car accident or a hard fall/accident to the head. The fact that Uranus is involved this suggests an injury that could have long term effects of a traumatic nature that impact the overall nervous system.

"The brain stem is an important part of the hindbrain, and it controls functions that are critical to life, such as breathing and swallowing. The cerebellum is also located here, playing a role in physical ability. The brain stem is a structure that connects the brain to the spinal cord. Damage to this structure can be catastrophic, as it controls such things as blood pressure, heartbeat, and swallowing." (Rad)

The type of injury is going to affect how the brain sends messages to the entire body including how the person is experiencing the pain resulting from the injury. In some cases this could feel like being plugged into a light socket of pain or the pain could shoot in out of nowhere. Also this signature connects to having a constant inner buzzing like static in the cells due to the nerves in the spinal column being traumatized or stressed. Because so much energy, blood, thus oxygen is being directed to the area of the potential injury, other organs could be also impacted if they are not getting the blood flow they need to perform efficiently.

Headaches caused by constant stress: Any form of

emotional stress caused by unresolved trauma will take its toll physically on the body for emotional stress is the root of all dis-ease.

Migraines: A migraine is a severe, painful headache that is often preceded or accompanied by sensory warning signs such as flashes of light, blind spots, tingling in the arm. Migraine headaches result from a combination of blood vessel enlargement and the release of chemicals from nerve fibers that coil around these blood vessels. During the headache, an artery enlarges that is located on the outside of the skull just under the skin of the temple (temporal artery). This causes a release of chemicals that cause inflammation, pain, and further enlargement of the artery.

Uranus connects to the LUNGS and the function of breathing so within this signature it could also connect to injury to the lungs for example a gunshot to the lungs or a puncture such as the rib puncturing the lung through some kind of accident. Also the predisposition to lung conditions such as Pneumonia which is caused by an inflammation of one or both lungs due to infection. Also Pleurisy which is an inflammation of the pleura, which is the moist, double-layered membrane that surrounds the lungs and lines the rib cage. The condition can make breathing extremely painful causing a sharp Mars pain when breathing, so with each breath, Uranus, there is a sharp Mars pain. Sometimes it is associated with another condition called pleural effusion, in which excess fluid fills the area between the membrane's layers.

PTSD is a Uranian phenomenon, Uranus also connects to the lungs and breathing, and as a result the stress can lodge itself in the lungs, similar to watching an accident happen, it creates one to gasp and the lungs freeze, you might find yourself holding your breath. All the oxygen exchanges occur in the lungs so if someone is not able to fully utilize lung capacity due to stress or not being able to breathe full or deeply, this then effects how oxygen it carried throughout the entire body thus how all of the organs are functioning for Oxygen equals LIFE.

Asthma: The airways are persistently inflamed, and may occasionally spasm, causing wheezing and shortness of breath. Asthma can manifest in Souls with unresolved trauma.

Because Mars connects to blood flow, as well as Mars ruling male genitalia, this could impact this man's ability to have an erection either through some trauma to his penis or as a result of nerve damage to the nerves that innervate this area.

Interruption of the flow .. short circuiting .. Uranus ruling the middle layer of the root chakra where the root of kundalini/sexual desires emanate can create a short circuiting because of the injury .. this could also reflect in a "healthy" body quite the opposite, an easy and fast and electric ease of being able to have erection .. being that it is an extreme signature...so in a healthy body it would not take any warming up.

With Mars oppose Uranus this can be linked with an extremity of adrenaline due to the sustained stress in some cases this can cause an Adrenaline Rush. When that rush kicks in it turns off bodily functions such as digestion and boosts oxygen and glucose to the brain.

This signature can also be linked with an extremity in acids as Mars rules all the acids in the body with Pluto which can therefore ignite digestive complications, as well as reflux whereby the stomach acids recede into the esophagus and cause a burning. This is known as GERD Gastroesophageal reflux disease that effect the lower esophageal sphincter. Esophagus is Mars.

The Mars oppose Uranus can also connect to PTSD combined with an intense of anger because of the traumas that may have occurred. The Mars oppose Uranus can also reflect a war symbol, being involved in explosions, gun shots etc. and so the trauma linked with war/anger/revolt will physically take its toll on the body especially as over the years, any long term memories of the war are released within the nervous system can create an emergence of anger and total panic to surface seemingly out of nowhere and the Mars, fight or flight, 3rd chakra ruler can create an intensity that causes the blood to boil and the heart to race effecting directly the heart muscle, adding extra stress to all of the capillaries, and blood vessels causing inflammation, stress to all organs.

At bare minimum this signature suggests a constant undercurrent of anxiety of some form that is always in place, never really free from stress, and the body always in a state of tension.

CHART A – Potential medical issues of Mars in opposition to Uranus in a male body

Practice Chart by Ari Moshe

Neurotransmitter acetylcholine is co-ruled by Uranus and

Mars as it is a neuro-transmitter that binds with skeletal muscle fibers. Upon binding to these fibers it opens up channels in the cell membranes which is then entered by sodium which apparently results in muscle contraction (the role of an electrolyte?). One correlation I can see from that is where the brain will fire the acetylcholine neurotransmitter due to some sort of fight flight response which results in involuntary muscle contraction/muscle tension.

Mars rules the testes and the penis. Acetylcholine is also responsible for the swelling of the penis, which correlates as well to the contraction of the testes. I imagine due to sexual trauma/sexual violence there can be issues with the firing or the reception of this neurotransmitter resulting in impotence and psychologically dissociative behavior around sexual arousal/expression of desires. Uranus also co-rules the sheathing on the nerves. There can be a wear on the nerve sheathing which then could eventually lead to nerve damage.

Dehydration throughout the body in general is possible with this opposition. I see that there are several kinds of dehydration. Most forms of dehydration in humans are isotonic which refers to an equal loss of water and electrolytes. This can be created through a great amount of stress on the central nervous system.

Mars rules red blood cells. Red blood cells are responsible for carrying lots of oxygen throughout the body. From wiki on red blood cells: "Red blood cells, or erythrocytes, are the most common type of blood cell and the vertebrate organism's principal means of delivering oxygen (O2) to the body tissues via the blood flow through the circulatory system. They take up oxygen in the lungs or gills and release it while squeezing through the body's capillaries."

The oxygen is received from the lungs which of course receives it from the air that is breathed. Lungs correlate to Uranus, and there can often be issues with full breathing due to various traumas. This can then have the impact of lowering the amount of oxygen in the blood which then effects the functioning of the entire body, including level of alertness/awakeness. This can lead to various medication conditions wherein the body is deprived of the oxygen that it needs. Of course there can also be difficulty breathing and there is the clear possibility of accidents/direct trauma involving the lungs as well which can affect all that was stated above. Injuries to the nose that impede upon the ease of taking in oxygen.

CHART A – Potential medical issues of Mars in opposition to Uranus in a male body

Practice Chart by Linda

Some correlations:

Uranus: brain, neurotransmitters, entire central nervous system, bursting action.

Mars: muscles, red blood cells, primary brain.

The specific correlation to the Mars opposite Uranus aspect is the severe disruption to the neurotransmitter, Acetylcholine, located in both the central nervous system (Uranus) and the peripheral nervous system (Uranus). In the central nervous system, acetylcholine plays a role in attention and arousal. In the peripheral nervous system, this neurotransmitter is a major part of the autonomic nervous system and works to activate muscles (Mars).

Neurotransmitters (Uranus) are chemical messengers which the brain (Uranus) uses to deliver instructions from one neuron (nerve cell) to another (the sheathing on the nerves correlates to Uranus). Without this versatile troupe working in concert, our brains could not function. Acetylcholine is a key player in this troupe. The body uses more of it than any other neurotransmitter.

Acetylcholine is the primary neurotransmitter in charge of muscle movement (Mars). It is found both in smooth muscle and skeletal muscle. Acetylcholine dictates that our muscles work in harmony. For mental alertness, concentration and memory, acetylcholine is a must. When levels are right, mood is elevated, the mind is focused, and intelligence increased. The brain performs its dance smoothly and effortlessly. When acetylcholine levels are low, learning and recall can plummet. The ability to think clearly and coherently can be disrupted.

This neurotransmitter also plays a vital role in controlling primitive drives and emotions, eg anger, fear, and aggression. When there is an imbalance among our neurotransmitters, these drives and emotions, now unchecked, can wreak havoc on both the individual affected and on the people around them.

Our brain's ability to create acetylcholine lessens as we get older. This can give rise to memory loss and possibly to dementia later in life. Research has shown that all people who experience dementia suffer from insufficient acetylcholine.

Steady blood flow (Mars, red blood cells) is vital for acetylcholine to do its job. But if blood flow in the brain is restricted, by damage caused by strokes, for example, acetylcholine takes a serious hit. This problem is compounded by the fact that the acetylcholine system controls blood flow to the outer portion of the brain. Uranus correlates with the brain (and Mars to the head), therefore strokes/injury within the brain, and to the physical action of bursting when an existing restriction within the body has reached an extreme.

A stroke is the rapidly developing loss of brain functions due to a disturbance in the blood vessels supplying blood to the brain. This can be due to ischemia (lack of blood supply) or to a hemorrhage (Uranus, bursting action). As a result, the affected area of the brain is unable to function. The ability of the brain to recover from such injury as stroke or trauma depends on a particular circuitry of neurons that 'talk' to one another using the brain chemical acetylcholine. Parasympathetic nerve fibers send out acetylcholine which induces relaxation, ie slows down the heart. In regards to the cardiac cycle, it influences the volume of blood (Mars) that is ejected during the cycle. When heart rate decreases, cardiac output should also decrease.

CHART A – Potential medical issues of Mars in opposition to Uranus in a male body

Practice Chart by Gonzalo

Possible manifestations include:

* stress, potential PTSD, and potential bursting involving the nervous system, potentially affecting the integrity of the myelin sheathing of neurons. Imbalances in the levels of neurotransmitters serotonin, and acetylcholine.

* Mars co-ruling acetylcholine and ruling adrenaline and muscles in general would create cycles of restlessness and muscular tension because of defensive physiological response, increased levels of lactic acid, and fluctuating levels of energy.

* also, potential irregular breathing, ranging from hyperventilation to shallow breathing or no breathing, affecting the levels of oxygen in the bloodstream

* heat in the lungs, and hemoptysis

* potential imbalances in the levels of iron and hemoglobin affecting oxygen/energy

* this is a potential signature for anemia

* potential de-hydration and fluctuating levels of testosterone, translating in fluctuating sexual desire.

* extremes in energy levels within the nervous system could produce a stroke

* tension in the diaphragm and the esophagus

* in some cases, the Uranus/Mars opposition could reflect a potential for diseases of sexual transmission affecting the nervous system* at the chakra system, Mars opposed Uranus could reflect an intention to align egocentric will with a higher will, which has required a liberation from Saturn conditioning. Thus, contents emanating from the individuated subconscious would be demanding externalized action

reflecting the liberation, with the potential for willful assertion at an egocentric level, with the underlying intention to align with a higher will, thus creating clashes of will. This will be different in each case and would depend on the evolutionary state of the individual.

* because the umbilical chakra relates to digestion, and the root chakra relates to elimination, the Uranus/Mars opposition could affect peristalsis and hydration of the gastrointestinal tract, producing constipation alternating with diarrhea.

CHART A – Potential medical issues of Mars in opposition to Uranus in a male body

Practice Chart by Upasika

Generally speaking there may be too much (opposition) electrical energy entering into the nervous system (Uranus), and this could cause restlessness, and combined with the Mars opposition impatience, which may lead to cuts, burns and other accidents.

The person will be prone to sporadic muscle rhythm because of excitability (Uranus), which in turn could lead muscular spasms at times. Mars relates to matters connected to the head skeleton, and Uranus to unpredictable movement which could lead to head injuries.

There could also be problems with overstimulated (Mars) nerves (Uranus) – twitching, nervousness, or nervous compression within some muscles leading to numbness, or "pins and needles."

The person will have an inherently charged energy system, as the testosterone production (Mars) will be strong. There could also be high levels of adrenaline produced, and the two in combination could lead to overly high exertion over an extended period of time (eg overwork, fighting), leading to adrenal burnout.

This in turn would produce excessive acidity in the body, which would lay the foundation for all manner of illnesses to manifest at some point in the future. Additionally Uranus under stress (opposition) would probably produce excessive free radicals. As the acid conditions would inhibit antioxidants that could neutralize those free radicals this would set up a generally disease prone bodily environment.

Mars is fiery which could aggravate the tendency of Uranus to produce dehydration, so they would need to drink plenty of fluids to make sure their body generally functioned and excreted well. They would also need to drink plenty of water to keep the serotonin levels up, which would help keep them calm.

Because Uranus rules the lungs and oxygen, and Mars the red blood cells that carry the oxygen around the body, this person may be prone to cigarette smoking, especially to settle their nerves and/or if there was no suitable physical outlet for their physical and emotional energy. Also there would be a tendency to excessive internal inflammation (Mars) as a result of all the above.

Practice Charts

STEP 2

So we can now move to our next step which is to place the Uranus/Mars opposition in a specific house. So let's put Uranus in the 4th house, and Mars in the 10th. When you refer to the correlations that have been provided focus on the sign Cancer and the 4th house, and Saturn and the 10th house. These houses now correlate to not only the type of inner and outer conditions that can serve to ignite the inherent potentialities of the Mars opposed Uranus, but also add to what those potentialities may be as defined by the houses that this aspect takes place within.

Practice Charts by

- Cat
- Skywalker
- Katherine
- Kristin
- Ari Moshe
- Gonzalo

CHART B – Potential medical issues of Mars in the 10th house in opposition to Uranus in the 4th house

Practice Chart by Cat

Here we have a man who potentially suffers from chronic stress or trauma due to parental and social conditioning patterns that make him believe that in order to be accepted, he must abide by the norms of society and work hard to get ahead and achieve a position of social status. Pressure from his parents and society cause him to work hard in order to climb the corporate ladder and be "successful." His need and desire to achieve does not allow him to relax as he believes he has to work hard in order to gain peer recognition and parental and social approval. He is driven to achieve. With Uranus in the 4th, the parental conditioning patterns are very strong as Uranus correlates to the mid layer of the root chakra which correlates to the "messaging" taking place within his entire body. Whatever he was conditioned to believe, permeates every cell in his body. In other words, his thoughts and beliefs, have a great deal of influence on his physical health. With Uranus in the 4th, there is a desire to break free and liberate himself from parental conditioning patterns, but they are so strong that this desire creates a great deal of stress and tension within him.

The 4th house correlates to the 3rd Eye Chakra which correlates to the pineal gland. It is very possible that this man suffers from migraine headaches due to the stress and tension from wanting to just be himself but being conditioned to be who and what his parents conditioned him to be. In addition he may have a hard time concentrating and suffer from confusion and negative feelings. Other potential physical problems include brain tumors, stroke, neurological problems such as Parkinson's, seizures, spinal difficulties, and problems with the ears, eyes, and nose.At the same time, Mars correlates to the Naval Chakra and the 10th house to the outer layer of the Root Chakra. When stressed or over worked, it is possible that this man becomes angry and possibly violent. Imbalances and stress can lead to tiredness or exhaustion, blood disorders, impotency, kidney or bladder problems, constipation, anemia, obesity, or lower back pain. And of course, anger can lead to accidents.

CHART B – Potential medical issues of Mars in the 10th house in opposition to Uranus in the 4th house

Practice Chart by Skywalker

As stated earlier, one of the key factors in this combination that can lead to medical issues is stress, with Uranus in the fourth house opposite Mars in the tenth house we now have more information relative to the inner and outer conditions that may lead to medical issues.

As Uranus is in the Fourth house, there can be subconscious memories of traumatic experiences from previous lives of abandonment or emotional shocks deep within the memory of the Soul, causing irrational or subconscious fears because of these memories. These experiences can also be re-played in the current life. Dynamics relative to emotional security, nurturing himself and others or, others nurturing him, can be stressful because of the need to rebel against crystalized emotional and family dynamics, that do not nurture and support a true representation of his individuality. The evolutionary intention is to accelerate his evolution by gaining objective awareness of his individual emotional security needs and to minimize external dependencies, therefore he may have to stand back as a group of one within his own family.

This person might grow up in a family environment where many of his personal needs would be unmet or his individuality simply misunderstood by the parents. Or certain dynamics within the family could be opposite what others of like mind expect from a "normal" household, making him feel like the only "normal" one in the environment by adhering to social values other than the familial ones. Physical and emotional violence in the family environment are also a possibility with the opposition to Mars because of these dynamics that can lead to polarized confrontations with the parents or others in authority or in the environment.

All this leads to a highly charged emotional energy in his life and environment that can make him very sensitive/defensive when threatened, snapping back impulsively and possibly having violent reactions. Others in the environment can also display this behavior by pushing him away/shocking him emotionally, with the effect of throwing him back on himself for his security needs instead of clinging on someone or something external. As emotional or even physical needs are potentially unmet, even from a very young age, the child is forced back upon himself for nurturing and emotional self-reliance.

This can lead to a sense of isolation and an inability to integrate emotionally within the family environment as a child, to become a rebel or a "problem child" that rejects everything out of a subconscious fear of losing his individuality to that which he is rebelling against. As an adult there can be an inability to relate emotionally with others in a consistent way, thus effecting their intimate and professional relationships by projecting security needs onto partners, expressing displaced emotions or being immature and irresponsible.

Consistency is needed for any living being to have a healthy emotional life and be a productive member of society. Without a solid, consistent, emotional sense of security and a healthy self-image, one cannot operate in society in a constructive, balanced manner. The opposition aspect shows the tension and difficulty in balancing the need for a healthy emotional life where he can express his individuality consistently, with a career and sense of social accomplishment.

With Mars in the Tenth house there can be the instinctive impulse to get ahead within the social scheme of whatever society the person finds himself in. Mars here will correlate to a person who acts in a goal oriented manner, with the tendency to be very ambitious. This ambition can be caused by the individuals need to learn self-responsibility from a young age, to fend for himself, to have to work hard in order to gain the approval/affection of authority figures, and due to dynamics shown by the opposition to Uranus, which can ignite the desire to break free from the family and be independent financially by working in the "real world", so he can be free to be himself.

The desire to get ahead and achieve goals can create stress/ frustration/anger as he encounters limitations from authority figures or other external or internal limiting factors. Mars in the Tenth can suppress emotional or physical needs in order to act responsibly and achieve set goals or to behave in the correct manner as defined by parents, society or external authority figures. This in itself can lead to inner frustration because of the suppression of natural desires in order to be in conformity with what is expected of him. When natural desires would be acted upon, to the contrary of what is "socially correct", there can be the fear of judgment from others, creating an inner feeling of man-made guilt.

Negative emotions such as guilt, fear, anger, frustration, anxiety and traumas that are unprocessed or suppressed, stay in the energetic/emotional bodies and affect him on a subconscious level. These emotions build up as energy blocks in the root, navel and ajna chakras effecting his sense of security, his will power and his perception. Because of his security needs (root) there can be a collision of wills which depletes his will power (navel), that has the effect of distorting his perception (ajna).

These dynamics can lead to the medical conditions mentioned earlier by all in this thread and to: Eating disorders or improper dietary practices. Contraction of the muscles due to emotional shock and/or emotional suppression which, if not relaxed can develop into contractures and possibly scoliosis. Tendinitis from working too hard in strenuous positions, osteoarthritis, muscle cramps. Anemia from mal nutrition, low calcium levels leading to low bone density, increasing the risks of osteoporosis which leads to weak bones that fracture easily.

Ulcers from suppressed negative emotions/excessive anxiety etc., digestive problems, acid reflux, heartburn. Poor nutrition leading to overall PH being too acidic which facilitates the development of bacteria in the body, causes lactic acid buildup, negative effect on immune system, joint inflammation, rheumatoid arthritis.

Poor vision from emotional trauma, dehydration, malnutrition, over straining the muscles and nerves in the eyes. This could correlate with glaucoma due to excessive water pressure/build-up in the system caused by stress. Eye twitches, dry eyes. Brain damage from mothers negative emotions while still in the womb, mothers diet, unhealthy habits such as smoking which limits the supply of oxygen to the unborn baby or trauma to the mother while pregnant. Difficult/traumatic childbirth for mother and or baby.

Serotonin imbalance leading to depression, erratic mood swings, insomnia, fatigue. Teeth grinding as a way for the body to release stress. Polycythemia, a bone marrow disease that over produces red blood cells and thickens the blood, causing clots that can lead to strokes or heart attack. Overactive bladder caused by neurological disorders, urinary incontinence due to weak muscles in the pelvic area. Dry scalp. Nervous breakdowns. Nervous ticks. ADHD. Multiple sclerosis? All sorts of accidents.

CHART B – Potential medical issues of Mars in the 10th house in opposition to Uranus in the 4th house

Practice Chart by Katherine

Mars in the 10th: This man would attract/pursue work environments that are intense (exposure to risk) and demand ambition. He would be very strong, naturally, and would have measure of his physical limits—at the same time, possessing an inclination to push them (Mars having traction in cardinal earth). He could come across as being provocative in the sense (gleam in the eye, so to speak) of being ready to 'step' (ie fight) and capable of doing damage. This underscores the previous notes about volatility. Intense physical activity might be an outlet for excess energy.

Perhaps climbing or weight lifting as a practical means of building form (Saturn) which could be a healthy way toward dealing with stress or, become a separating desire to be recognized, objectified, feared. (Cardinal ref. to Cancerian insecurity and Libran aesthetics). Either way, the tendency toward competitiveness, independence, domination channeled through feats of strength and endurance would create stress to musculoskeletal system. Positively, this would increase blood circulation (O2) and bone density.

Negatively, lactic acid accumulation in the muscles would aggravate an already acidic pH, overall. Overriding signals of strain and fatigue (singular focus on desire - Mars) would lead to injury. Adhesions between the layers of tissues would create any number of soft tissue ailments.

Other issues: facial trauma (Bell's palsy) clenching jaw, grinding teeth at night, TMJ, tension headaches, hyperthyroid-increased heart rate, palpitation, tremors, anxiety, elevated blood pressure/hypertension (hyper vigilant sympathetic nervous system), inflammation, eg (osteo) arthritis, (chronic) joint pain, cracking/popping in joints, acid reflux, tightness in upper trapezius (specifically links to stress / the gut via Uranus in 4th). Possible distorted desires for sexual domination, there's room here too for repression/self-criticism and judgment of these desires which, would manifest into physical disease mostly related to stagnation of blood (clots, etc.) displaced anger, and in extreme cases of psycho-sexual disorder: forced sex/rape.

Massage modalities: active isolated stretching and myofascial release to keep muscles tracking correctly. Asana: standing posture emphasizing balance, muscular, and organic energy connect navel and root chakras, eg Virabhadrasana I,*II*,III, and Bhujangasana to ground

Uranus in the 4th: This man would have an obtuse yet core sense of alienation, not feeling at home within the home/body due to possible early trauma with a general heightened (live wire) sense of insecurity relative to personal safety. They would have a short fuse and an elevated instinct when around others to filter all sensory data for potentially harmful or physically threatening circumstances (inconjunct from Cancer to Aquarius). Paraverbal communication is noticed, details (punctuated by smell) are remembered with minimal reminder to recall.

Over worked sympathetic, underutilized parasympathetic system. (Reinforces above signature, taxing kidneys/adrenals) This is not to say "paranoid" but, very watchful. This vigilance and emotional stress takes its toll on the stomach by way of a feeling of 'gut rot,' nausea/unsettled leads to disinterest/ aversion to eating food which would create chemical imbalances (supplement B vitamins) and more disorders. Intermittent digestive issues (IBS) disruption to pH regulation, enzyme production, which can cause gas/bloating which leads to blockages that then cause autointoxication. Then painfully (possibly explosive) diarrhea would further create a situation of dehydration. Ulcers likely.

Other Issues: dry eyes and/or sensitivity to prolonged exposure of sunlight, night driving, or TV/computer monitor. congenital neurological disorder: Uranus seems infused by a watery 4th house so no comment on the myelin or any other insulators, yet.

Massage modalities: chi nei tsang, thai

Asana: most twists, supta virasana, ustrasana, urdhva dhanurasana (when well) setu bandha sarvangasana

To me, the Uranus-Mars opposition has been reinforced by the house placement of 4-10, respectively. On one side, a capability to endure (and thrive) under physical strain and on the other, a delicate constitution that requires time, rest, and care. Spartan meets Goldilocks? Balancing the two would be a challenge that may mean very separate times to engage fully in both dynamics of energy moving out and energy moving in, ie work out early in the morning and at night take it easy with alkalizing foods and plenty of time to unplug and relax. Either way, two basic things are crucial: water (with an alkalizer: lemon or coconut) and sleep in very dark, quiet, and safe environments to recharge.

CHART B – Potential medical issues of Mars in the 10th house in opposition to Uranus in the 4th house

Practice Chart by Kristin

Considering Mars represents the lead point in a Soul's evolution, for the Soul to choose to come into a life with Mars in the 10th, this would signify a Soul who has chosen to shoulder a great deal of responsibility, a natural leader, a warrior in some cases as in a modern day soldier, a head of a corporation, perhaps self-owned and or a president or senator. Regardless, they would carry a great feeling and burden of responsibility. Mars in the 10th oppose Uranus could also mean a Soul who was forced to grow up fast or to take responsibility at a young age. He may have been left home alone while the parent(s) worked. Of course we need to look at the entire chart nevertheless, the burden of responsibility is there. This signature might also reflect broken family structure when the Soul was young as in divorce or losing one or both parents and being raised by extended family, possibly adoption, which would have taken a toll on the Soul emotionally.

Mars in 10th oppose Uranus in 4th further reflects potentially a Soul in a past life defending his homeland and the trauma that occurred as a result, perhaps he himself dying while defending his family. The opposition to Uranus reflects watching loved ones perish and the PTSD that ensued the inability to access emotions as emotions and overreaction to the slightest emotional outbursts rage linked with fear or someone who has simply seen too much.

A common theme for all Souls is the need to feel secure. With Mars in the 10th opposing Uranus in the 4th this reflects unexpected events that totally devastate that feeling of security where the Soul feels totally emotionally anxious and inwardly traumatized and alone. Also as I mentioned in a prior post, the inability to ever emotionally relax. This can translate into chronic anxiety, in some cases panic and also chronic depression (10th).

Uranus with the Moon also rules the Hypothalamus with is a portion of the brain which directs a multitude of important functions including regulating the endocrine system. The endocrine system is the system of glands, each of which secretes different types of hormones directly into the bloodstream (some of which are transported along nerve tracts) to maintain homeostasis. With Mars opposing Uranus in the 4th this would suggest the potential for the hormones to be out of balance and hormones regulate various human functions, including metabolism, growth and development, tissue function, sleep, and mood.

Mars in the 10th - physical structure of the body including the entire skeleton, opposing Uranus in the 4th can equal experiencing a sudden injury, possibly being in an explosion for example in war or at battle or an accident occurring at home, 4th house. This could also signify being in a fire at home. This signature might reflect someone who could have even become blind in an explosion as Cancer 4th house, Moon connects to the eyes. Other possibilities with the eyes are cataracts which forms naturally as one ages, 10th house, and glaucoma. Glaucoma refers to a group of diseases that cause damage to the optic nerve, Uranus. If left untreated, glaucoma may cause vision loss and blindness.

Mars in the 10th opposing Uranus in the 4th could signify an overly acidic stomach, acid indigestion, also reflux known as GERD, Gastro esophageal reflux disease is an acid reflux disease is a chronic symptom of mucosal damage caused by stomach acid coming up from the stomach into the esophagus. Gerd is chronic symptom of mucosal (Mars in the 10th)damage. GERD is usually caused by changes in the barrier between the stomach and the esophagus, including abnormal relaxation of the lower esophageal sphincter, which normally holds the top of the stomach closed impaired expulsion of gastric reflux from the esophagus, or a hiatal hernia. These changes may be permanent or temporary. Unresolved emotions and anger can fester in the belly, also experiences of massive stress and danger can result of an endorphin surge from unresolved rage stirring in the guts which impacts digestion. This could be a Soul with so much repressed emotion and not vehicle for release that the energy turns on itself .. inverts .. and the result is would poor digestion to reflux to the feeling of inflamed guts, like a belly on fire. Mars in the 10th opposing Uranus in the 4th could connect to inflammation of the lining of the belly. Also this would increase the propensity for stomach ulcers which is most commonly caused to high amounts of stress.

Head injury to the occipital lobe..(4th) which is the most posterior part of the back of the head .. could have slipped and fell back on head .. or a fall from high up such as someone falling off a roof of a house, structure 10th, home 4th. Also paralysis in extreme cases where the spinal cord, Uranus is injured/severed. The spinal cord is the elongated bundle of nervous tissue that carries nerve impulses between the brain and the rest of the body. It lies in the vertebral canal of the vertebral column, this connects to Saturn/10th house.

Ultimately this would be a Soul who is under so much emotional stress due whether as a result of responsibilities they have taken on in the world, or constantly worrying about their family, 4th house, perhaps they have long term memories in some cases of trauma to loved ones and it makes it impossible for them to ever relax. These memories may also simply be deep in their cellular memory and it creates an undercurrent of unrelenting persistent anxiety, and the Soul may be unaware of why and where it is coming from if it is from a past life. Or there may have been traumas as a child that the Soul has consciously 'forgotten' attempted to detach from in order to protect themselves. This signature could also connect to some form of child abuse, sexual and/or physical, by the mother and perhaps an angry father with elements of rage in the home. This may also reflect an upbringing where the emotions of the parents were repressed or parents that were emotionally distant.

The cingulate cortex, Uranus, is a part of the brain situated in the medial aspect of the cerebral cortex. It includes the cortex of the cingulate gyrus (Uranus withe the Moon -4th house). The cingulate cortex. It is an integral part of the limbic system, which is involved with emotion formation and processing, learning, and memory. The combination of these three functions makes the cingulate gyrus highly influential in linking behavioral outcomes to motivation. This role makes the cingulate cortex highly important in disorders such as depression and schizophrenia. It also plays a role in executive function and respiratory control.

The causes of schizophrenia have been the subject of much debate, with various factors proposed and discounted or modified. Studies suggest that genetics, prenatal development, early environment, neurobiology and psychological and social processes are important contributory factors which can be reflected in with Mars in the 10th opposing Uranus in the 4th house.

With Uranus ruling the respiratory system and the lungs, the Mars in the 10th opposing Uranus in the 4th could signify shallow breathing due to the ongoing emotional stress and fears lodged in the lungs as well as asthma. Specific allergies and asthma may be a result of unresolved trauma from the past and a predisposition for pneumonia or pleurisy.

Mars in the 10th oppose Uranus could also connect to the Soul getting Parkinson's disease as one ages, 10th house. a common neurologic disease believed to be caused by deterioration of the brain cells that produce dopamine, occurring primarily after the age of 60, characterized by tremors, Uranus. My mom was diagnosed at 79 with Parkinson's as she has a Mars oppose Uranus aspect although not in the 4th and the 10th, however they do square her 10th house Pluto in Cancer which correlates to the same archetypes here.

Also another possibility as he ages, 10th house Mars would be dementia or Alzheimer's, with the opposition to Uranus, which involves a progressive decline, changes in the brain, in the aging process impacting memory, including not recognizing members of their own family, 4th house.

The relative degree of possibilities within this aspect can be reflected in the level of emotional repression of emotion, Mars in the 10th, and the trauma seen in the opposition to Uranus in the 4th, that would throw this Soul back upon itself in order to evolve.

CHART B – Potential medical issues of Mars in the 10th house in opposition to Uranus in the 4th house

Practice Chart by Ari Moshe

So basic correlations with Mars in the 10th house, just by itself can imply an individual that might be very strong. Muscles that connect to the bones, as well as the bones, correlate to Saturn. Mars is muscles as well. So there can be a strong structure to this body.

Taking Uranus in the 4th just by itself, since the 4th house

correlates to all containers in the body and Uranus correlates to "bursting" when an existing limitation has reached a restriction, there can be issues with holding on to urine due to unresolved childhood trauma, leading to a bursting of the bladder. With Mars in opposition in the 10th house, we can also see a strain on the muscles that would be involved in contracting the bladder, which can lead to things like ruptures of some sort. Rupturing can occur within the anal canal as well.

Along with the possibility of trauma linked with sexual function, now we see that there may be a repression/holding back of sexual desire due to unresolved emotional trauma and guilt linked to the sexual function. This holding back of the sexual impulse - especially if during sex - can lead to a buildup of semen which creates stress on the testes which can result in a bladder infection, or injure/weaken the muscle that is responsible for ejaculation. Something can rupture as well. There can be injuries to the nose, 10th house, Uranus, which leads to an impediment of air flow, which leads to a lack of oxygen going to the brain which leads to a decrease in concentration. Difficulty in breathing can lead to cramping and pain in the stomach and an overall poor ability to digest food. All this can lead to pain in the spine in various places. Due to conditioned emotional responses, this individual may perpetuate stress in the body and the alignment of the spine by creating forceful and compulsive movements such as compulsively cracking the neck or spine when nervous or under emotional stress.

Since Mars rules the naval Chakra and we're looking at its placement in the 10th house opposite Uranus there may be repression of basic urges, which then leads to a holding back of his fire which can translate to weak digestion. This can lead to inflections in various organs in the body. There may be issues with elimination here as well, Saturn root chakra along with the anal canal. The Moon correlates to the third eye, there may be great psychic sensitivity to his surroundings - due to being very sensitive, this Soul may be on guard all the time, on emotional defense - this can lead to high blood pressure (is this true?) and other conditions I stated above such as issues with elimination, bursting or hemorrhaging of organs as a result of creating so much internal stress. The third eye correlation of the Moon along with Uranus in the 4th correlating to so many parts of the brain, and migraines in general, there can be strong headaches that are set off by various stress stimuli.

CHART B – Potential medical issues of Mars in the 10th house in opposition to Uranus in the 4th house

Practice Chart by Gonzalo

* An Intensified signature of stress and/or potential PTSD, connecting to prior lifetimes and/or early environment, a signature for potential early domestic violence, and child abuse ... probably not all cases, but perhaps most of them.

* Extreme intensity of emotional states thereof, because of the 4th House AND Uranus correlations with the Amygdala and the Cingulate Cortex, and the 4th House correlation with the Limbic system.

* Confirms Intensity of imbalances of neurotransmitter serotonin because of its correlation with Saturn/Uranus/Moon.

* The HPA system would be very implied, because of Uranus/4th House correlation with Hypothalamus, Pituitary correlation with Saturn (as well as Pluto and Jupiter) and Mars correlation with the adrenals.

* Potential 'breakdown in the integrity of the b and t cells that manifest from the bone marrow, which can then implicate immune system issues'. Also, the high levels of stress would directly impact on the immune system. 'Imbalance between the white and red blood cells'.

* Because it is a signature of potential fragmentation within personality (Uranus 4th House), it can correlate with what was called few years ago borderline personality disorder, the symbols correlating most cases with aspects of the personality defined by extremely intense emotions which are not integrated between them and within the personality.

* I am reasoning that these sole symbols can reflect either the potential for high levels of sustained stress, or the potential for PTSD (coming from childhood, from pre-natal life, or from prior lifetimes). The levels of cortisol secreted would tend to be extreme ... low, in case of PTSD, high in the case of sustained high stress (though, I note cortisol correlates with Venus, however, being a signature of stress, it seems to me it would be involved via the Uranus correlation...)

* Potential for memory issues or disorders, both in 'scene memory' associated with recognition of social context (10th House, Uranus/Saturn correlation with Parahippocampal gyrus), and face recognition (Uranus 4th House, I wonder the Fusiform face area would correlate with Uranus/Moon); also because the Cingulated cortex correlates with Uranus/Moon, being connected with emotion processing and memory; and further, because cortisol and adrenaline work together in creating short-term memories of emotional events, while long term levels of cortisol (as would be the case in sustained stress, versus PTSD) can damage cells in the Hippocampus-Uranus-impacting on memory and

learning.

* Because of the Cingulated cortex correlation with Uranus/Moon, and because it relates with emotion processing, memory, and learning, it is associated with motivation. Thus, Mars 10th House reflects potential for depression, and fatigue, chronic fatigue, fibromyalgia, irritability, 'sudden and unexpected bouts of anger' (I'm quoting Spiritual Anatomy of Emotion).

* The Amygdala is connected with regulation of fight/fly response (Uranus/Mars), and further, with regulation of 'temporary immobility before fight or flight', and thus, it can create a 'freezing' response in some cases (10th House Mars).

* I wonder that the Prefrontal lobe, and the Orbitofrontal cortex can correlate with Uranus/Saturn, thus, with Mars in the 10th these areas would be highly activated or imbalanced in some cases reflecting desires to maintain external controls, or on the contrary, desires to lose social control. Also the Basal ganglia could be involved, dealing with 'action selection' and motor inhibitory control, with Mars being in the 10th House, because of the Basal ganglia correlation with Uranus (however, co-ruled by Jupiter) .... this would reflect a conflict between First and Third chakras ... and the conflict between controlling and liberating of control would impact in the body movement, potentially creating neurological conditions such as Parkinson or Huntington's disease.

* In some cases, a potential for 'antisocial behavior' and aggression.

* Because of Saturn/Moon correlation with Calcium, and Saturn correlations with Magnesium and Phosphorus, and the 10th House correlation with the skeleton, and Mars/Saturn correlation with muscles (and Mars/Uranus correlation with acetylcholine, and Mars with adrenaline, affecting the tension or stiffness/softness of muscles) there would be a potential impact on the structure of the bones. Given that cortisol affects the absorption of Calcium, the case would be different depending on whether sustained stress or PTSD exist.

If sustained stress has existed since early childhood, there could be an impact of bone development and growth because of high levels of cortisol, leading to fragility of the bones, and osteoporosis.

* Because of 4th House correlation with stomach, and the umbilical and root chakras implied in digestion and elimination, the Uranus/ Mars opposition could manifest a series of digestive issues.

* Given the 4th House correlation with the eyes, and the Uranus/Moon correlation with the Occipital lobe dealing with visual processing, the Uranus/Mars opposition could affect vision. One way this could occur is through imbalances of the inner blood pressure in the eye, or through a stroke affecting the Occipital lobe.

MEDICAL ASTROLOGY

Practice Charts

STEP 3

Our next step will be to put the Uranus/Mars opposition in the 4th/10th Houses in a sign to determine additional psychological/ medical correlations: to see if in so doing there are more **potential** issues that may occur. So let's put Uranus in Virgo, and Mars in Pisces. What additional potentials could exist in so doing ?

Practice Charts by

- Kristin
- Skywalker
- Cat
- Katherine

CHART C – Potential medical issues of Mars in Pisces in The 10th house in opposition to Uranus in Virgo in the 4th House

Practice Chart by Kristin

Highly compromised immune system due to persistent emotional stress and trauma. Immune system connects to Neptune/Pisces and with ongoing repeated emotional stress this can wear down the immune system and cause an increased susceptibility to the body breaking down and getting sick.

Exposure to metals, Capricorn/10th house/Saturn

Imbalance of metals in the body.

Metals make vital functions like respiration, circulation and reproduction possible

Cobalt, for instance, found at the core of vitamin B12, is key to making red blood cells, while iron allows those cells to ferry oxygen and other important chemicals to the body's tissues. Calcium not only strengthens bones but also plays a role in muscle, nerve function and blood clotting. Sodium and potassium help the heart and nerves communicate through electrical signals.

Exposure to too much metal can be harmful. But not getting enough metal in the right places can make us sick, too. This is the case with conditions such as iron-deficiency anemia and osteoporosis.

Autism is a disorder of neural development characterized by impaired social interaction and verbal and non-verbal communication. Autistic children are known to express a lack of emotion but they are in fact highly emotional Souls. The inability to express this lack of emotion is due to unresolved trauma from another life. Uranus in Pisces in the 4th opposing Mars in Virgo in the 10th reflects this inability to express emote the emotion locked up within.

Mute - Mercury connects to the throat and throat chakra, Mercury rules Virgo. Uranus in Virgo opposing Mars can reflect the reason the Soul is mute is due to emotional trauma and this may also be sue to injury.

Loss of hearing due to an explosion. The anatomy of the ear connects with Mercury, Mercury being the ruler of Virgo.

Injury and/or trauma to the Spleen (Neptune) which helps to clean the blood and is part of the immune system. The contributes to the production and storage of blood cells as part of the circulatory system.

Injury and trauma, Uranus opposing Mars, to bones in the feet, Pisces

Poor circulation to the feet, which is often referred to as peripheral vascular disease, is the result of a lack of oxygenated blood being pumped to the extremities (feet - Neptune/Pisces and hands Mercury /Virgo) of the body. Poor circulation has several possible causes and risk factors and produces several distinctive symptoms.

Someone experiencing insufficient blood circulation to the feet may feel a variety of sensations, including numbness, tingling or the sensation of pins and needles. Peripheral arterial occlusion, or hardening of the arteries, can cause hands and feet to feel numb, tingly, heavy or tense. If these symptoms occur, along with pain or leg cramps from a short walk, poor concentration and memory, impotence or frigidity, it is advised to seek medical evaluation because hardening of the arteries is considered by many to be America's number one killer.

Buerger's disease, a condition brought on by chronic inflammation of the blood vessels in smokers, can also cause a tingling sensation in the toes. A number of other conditions can cause numbness in the feet, including diabetic neuropathy, multiple sclerosis, a pinched nerve, rheumatoid arthritis and stroke, according to Dr. James Balch, author of "Prescription for Nutritional Healing."

CHART C – Potential medical issues of Mars in Pisces in the 10th house in opposition to Uranus in Virgo in the 4th house

Practice Chart by Skywalker

Uranus in Virgo in the fourth house can be in a perpetual

state of **emotional crisis** repeated over and over again, with the consequence of traumatically fracturing the person mentally and emotionally. The person could have endured so much trauma/abuse/ridicule/criticism early on in this life or have subconscious memories of persecution and related dynamics from other lives, leading to a sense of inner paranoia and intense stress, which the person just wants to liberate from. The desire to liberate from intense and difficult emotional dynamics can lead the person to attempt to totally deny any type of vulnerability by denying any type of emotional expression or to express extremely intense emotions in unpredictable and defensive ways.

Respiratory conditions such as shallow breathing can be a reflection of the persons subconscious attempt **not to feel**. Simply a coping mechanism to deal with the emotional trauma endured. Habits such as smoking can also be formed by these same dynamics.

Uranus in Virgo in the 4th house points to trauma based on cyclical **crisis due to lack**, with quite a potential for violence when opposing Mars. This can be a lack of many things ranging from food, to emotional nurturing, care, education, etc. Again, this has the effect of forcing the child upon himself and only himself to learn lessons of emotional self-reliance and security from within. A psychological condition that may manifest as a result is an inferiority complex. Also many personality disorders could manifest, depending on other chart factors and/or his personal karma/choices.

This placement shows potential for a huge **inner void** relative to emotional dynamics, where the person feels an inability to integrate emotionally in life in general due to a fractured personality. Eating disorders can be caused by this inner void, such as the desire to fill it up by over eating or being addicted to sugar or junk food. Another possibility is the attempt to always be busy one way or another in order to not face or fill up the inner void. This keeps the person in a perpetual state of crisis and as the crisis demands immediate attention, the person is simply avoiding the fact that there is an inner void.

All sorts of addictions and addictive behavior are a possibility with this planetary combo, including sexual addictions or alcoholism/ substance abuse.

As Mars is in Pisces, the stress that is created by these and other dynamics will have the effect of weakening the immune system, leaving the body susceptible to viral infections. High fevers are a possibility with this planetary combination as the body attempts to fight off viruses. Mars in Pisces opposing Uranus might also neglect its own needs or simply be oblivious to what to do in certain circumstances, thus not treating infections or colds properly, with the effect of them recurring and weakening the immune system even further while potentially damaging the lungs, trachea or bronchi. The **constant "fight or flight"** nature of this person is highly stressful, therefore also taxing the immune system. Mars in Pisces can also create all sort of fantasies and illusions that contribute to a state of depression when those illusions don´t pass the "acid test" and the individual is faced with a less than ideal reality.

Insomnia or other sleeping disorders are possible as Mars in Pisces correlates to the Pineal gland. The Pineal gland secretes Melatonin and is what regulates sleep, has antioxidant effects, has an effect on reproductive hormones. When the body does not rest well over a period of time due to Melatonin deficiency or other causes, there can be fatigue as a result, memory loss, depression, anxiety, loss of libido and a weakened immune system. Hypersensitivity to light due to Melatonin deficiency can cause severe headaches and migraines, the body may age faster as free radicals are not neutralized by antioxidants efficiently. Melatonin deficiencies may also contribute to neurodegenerative disorders such as Parkinson's, Alzheimer's, Multiple Sclerosis.

The Sympathetic/Parasympathetic nervous systems, also known as the Autonomic Nervous System, correlate to the Cancer, Virgo and Aquarius archetypes and respective houses and planets. Since there is stress between all the archetypes that correlate to this part of the nervous system, I would look there and to the whole nervous system for potential medical conditions. Also to the Limbic system for possible reasons for potential nervous conditions relative to emotional dynamics.

The ANS is a part of the nervous system that acts as a control system for the visceral functions of the body and regulates things like heart rate, perspiration, respiratory rate, salivation, sexual desire, digestion and more.

With this aspect there can be difficulty with the body regulating itself: for example a person who over perspires in situations where he gets nervous, or when in some sort of stressful situation one suddenly needs to use the toilet. If extreme, disorders of the ANS can become debilitating in many ways as the visceral functions that the ANS regulate can be easily thrown off balance by external stimulus or internal stress.

CHART C – Potential medical issues of Mars in Pisces in the 10th house in opposition to Uranus in Virgo in the 4th house

Practice Chart by Cat

Here we have a man who potentially suffers from chronic stress or trauma caused by parental and social conditioning patterns that have led him to believe that in order to be accepted by others, he must abide by the norms of consensus society and work long and hard in order to get ahead. He has been conditioned to believe that social status and his sociological role or career define who he is.

Pressure from his parents, culture, society, and his own inner voice, which is a reflection of his conditioning, cause him to excessively strive to be a "success." His need and desire to achieve does not allow him to relax as he believes he has to work hard in order to gain peer recognition and parental and social approval.

Mars correlates to the Naval Chakra and the 10th House to the outer layer of the Root Chakra. With Mars in Pisces in the 10th House opposition Uranus in Virgo in the 4th House, this man may suffer from emotional stress caused by a weak vitality coupled with a tendency to over work. Stress causes him to become angry and instead of expressing his anger, he allows it to boil up inside.

At key points in his life, he is likely to explode over some little thing that has nothing to do with what is really bothering him, which is his pent up anger that has been brewing within him for a very long time. He may become violent when he explodes or have an accident.

With Mars in Pisces, he may not possess a great deal of

energy and his vitality may be low. Imbalances and stress lead to tiredness or exhaustion, blood disorders, impotency, kidney or bladder problems, constipation, anemia, obesity, or lower back pain. He may be susceptible to sudden fevers, colds and flus throughout his life. He may suffer from a vitamin B deficiency as well.

There is the possibility that he may try to relax and relieve his stress through drugs or alcohol. Excessive drinking and alcoholism are strong possibilities and tie in with vitamin B deficiencies. These can lead to sugar aliments. Hyperinsulinism (above normal levels of insulin) is another possibility.

Uranus correlates to the mid layer of the root chakra which correlates to the "messaging" taking place within his entire body. Parental conditioning patterns are very strong and permeate every cell in his body. His thoughts and beliefs, which are a product of these parental conditioning patterns, have a great deal of influence on his physical health.

With Uranus in Virgo in the 4th House, this man has a strong desire to break free and liberate himself from the parental conditioning patterns that rule him. He tries to do so through his work and career but suffers from feelings of guilt when his desire to break free conflicts with the parental voices in his head. This produces a great deal of emotional stress and tension within him which has a negative impact on his health.

The 4th house correlates to the 3rd Eye Chakra which correlates to the pineal gland. He may suffer from migraine headaches due to the emotional stress and tension he experiences resulting from conflicting desires to be himself and to be the person his parents conditioned him to be. I addition, he is likely to have a hard time concentrating and suffer from confusion and negative feelings.

On a physical level, this can all lead to neurological problems including strokes and brain tumors. Parkinson's Disease, seizures, spinal difficulties, and problems with the ears, eyes, and nose are possibilities as well. In addition, severe emotional stress may lead to the sudden onset of diabetes or hypoglycemia. He may also suffer from intermittent sugar problems due to past life or early childhood trauma. Spasms and cramping in his intestinal tract are possibilities as well.

CHART C – Potential medical issues of Mars in Pisces in the 10th house in opposition to Uranus in Virgo in the 4th house

Practice Chart by Katherine

Uranus in Virgo in the 4th: I would say of Uranus (higher octave, fixed, air, yang) in Virgo (lower octave, mutable, earth, yin) that with the strong mercurial resonance—thinking, communicating, processing internal and external stimuli and emphasis of an inward context, in the 4th (cardinal, water, yin) that this combination would make for a highly self-critical, sensitive, and generally insecure individual. Specifically, on the mental and emotional levels, there could be an innate tendency toward avoidance, withdrawal, and disassociation. This could easily lead to substance abuse of depressants or hallucinogens as a way to self-medicate. Mental illness such as Borderline personality disorder reflects an unstable self-image, a sense of emptiness and inferiority, and a tendency to vacate. Mood disturbances such as 'splitting' (black and white thinking) peak in idealization and objectification, and pitch into devaluation and dismissal.

In extreme cases Schizophrenia where there are major imbalances of dopamine levels, also contributing to anxiety and depression. Delusions, disordered thoughts and speech, tactile, auditory, visual, olfactory, and hallucinations, typically regarded as manifestations of psychosis. Impairment of the hippocampus, frontal, and temporal lobes during fetal development is a possible cause. Hyperactive mental activity (depending on the structure of consciousness, relative intelligence, creative capacity, and familial support) could imply savant, high-functioning autism (Asperger's—restrictive and highly repetitive interests and behavior) prodigious, or precocious capabilities. Energetically, the root and third eye chakras would be affected, furthering a sense of confusion regarding identity and clear guidance from within. Physically, again stress, fatigue, difficultly resting, or dropping into REM sleep. Nervous ticks, twitches, shaky hands, headaches, ocular dehydration and degeneration.

Mars in Pisces in the 10th: Mars (cardinal, fire, yang) in Pisces (mutable, water, yin) in the 10th (cardinal, earth, yin) Again, a positive polarity planet in a yin sign and in a yin house ... and in opposition. So, there is a consistent tension—albeit the Uranus configuration is analogous through rulership, Mars via mode. This seems to echo a kind of disillusion, isolation, and suffering. Escape through fantasy, disassociation, and addiction. Confusion and loss of identity seemingly transcended (spiritualized) through entertainment, drugs and alcohol, disconnected sex. This reminds me of the riddle: what gets larger the more you take away? Perhaps there could be the possibility of being an inspired musician or artist, a visionary on some level? Dreams needing to be documented. I'm not sure why I can't think of a happy scenario for this man ... why I'm getting a sense of struggle. On the physical level, issues of the immune system and the blood, eg sickle-cell anemia, poor circulation, vasculitis, varicosity, thrombosis. The three lowest chakras (root, sacral, navel) would be prone to disrupting the others. This would be a conscious choice to engage in pranic breath, vipassana meditation, or other practices that are both invigorating and grounding.

CHART D – Uranus correlations – Parkinson's Disease

Uranus rules the mid brain with the Moon. Uranus also correlates to the neurotransmitter Dopamine. Parkinson's is a degenerative disorder of the central nervous system. The motor symptoms of Parkinson's disease result from the death of dopamine-generating cells in the region of the midbrain. Her natal Uranus is in Aries in the 7th house and inconjuncts her Moon in Scorpio in the 2nd house, and it is exact, reflecting this imbalance. Also her Pluto in Cancer in the 10th house, which is ruled by that Moon, and Pluto squares her Uranus in Aries.

Her disease was diagnosed when Pluto in Capricorn first squared Uranus in Aries in 2011. She was born when Pluto in Cancer was squaring Uranus in Aries and her disease manifested when Pluto was in Capricorn squaring Aries on the other side.

CHART E – Neptune correlations – imagining

The key here is Neptune: imagining. Example 1: Famous pianist Glenn Gould had South Node Virgo 3rd house, North Node Pisces 9th house, with Neptune/Jupiter Virgo conjunct

South Node, ruled by Mercury 4th house. He used a technique to develop his abilities by playing the piano in his mind, ie imagining the movement of the body. So, given that Mercury thought forms are directly linked with what the physical body can do, ie the immediate environment, such technique is based on Mercury, however, the coordination and integration functions are Jupiter correlations.

Example 2: Moshe Feldenkrais, whose method is based on exercises which are done on one side of the body, and then imagined for the other side of the body. His Nodal axis was Pisces/Virgo, and had Pluto in Gemini opposed by Uranus in Sagittarius, both squaring the Nodes.

CHART F – Albert Einstein

It is now a proven fact that the brain of Einstein was in fact not only larger than any other human, but that the vital corridor that connects the right and left brain hemispheres was itself extremely large. This is the area in the brain that synthesizes all the crossing information from the right and left brains in such a way as to intuitively see the larger picture of anything.

From his birth chart we can then all see how EA medical astrology perfectly reflects these facts. Consider the appropriate symbols such as his Jupiter in Aquarius in the 9th which is then ruled by his Uranus in Virgo in the 3rd, that his South Node of Mercury is conjunct that natal Jupiter, that his Jupiter is the natural ruler of his Sagittarius Moon which is conjunct the South Node of Uranus and Lucifer, God inspiration, the South Nodes of Vesta, Neptune, and Venus all in Aquarius, and that is natal Pluto, Ceres, Neptune, and Chiron are all in the 11th house.

MEDICAL ASTROLOGY

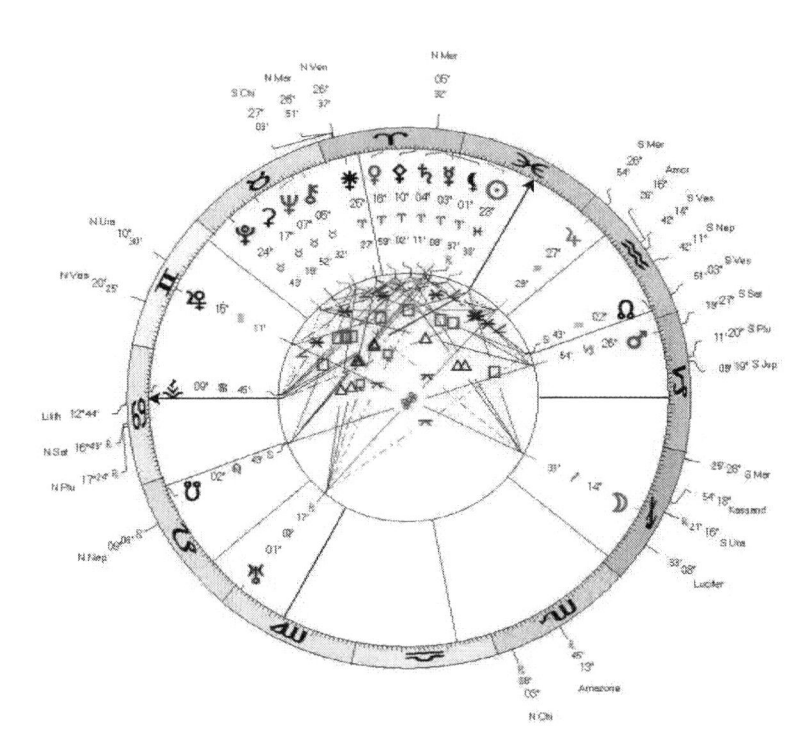

ALBERT EINSTEIN

6 MEDICAL ASTROLOGY CORRELATIONS

INDEX	
Acetylcholine	Uranus co-ruled with Mars
Acids (all acids) in the body	Mars with Pluto
Adipose tissue	Moon with Saturn and Pluto
Adrenal glands	Pluto co-ruled with Mars and Venus
Adrenaline	Mars
Adrenocorticotrophic hormone (ACTH)	Jupiter co-ruled with Saturn and Pluto
Aging of the body	Saturn
Amino acids (all)	Pluto

Amygdala	Mercury, Moon, Pluto, Uranus
Anal canal	Pluto co-ruled with Saturn
Angiotensinogen (hormone of the liver)	Jupiter
Anterior pituitary hormones	Jupiter co-ruled with Saturn and Pluto
Anti-diuretic hormone (ADH)	Moon with co-rulers Neptune and Jupiter
Arms and hands	Saturn co-ruled with Mercury
Arteries	Pluto co-ruled with Mars and Saturn
Arthritis	Saturn
Astral body	Neptune
Atrophy	Saturn
Awake, being	Neptune
Axons	Uranus

B cells (from bone marrow)	Saturn
Bacteria (all)	Pluto
Balance, sense of	Venus
Basal ganglia	Jupiter with Uranus
Betatrophin (hormone of the liver)	Jupiter
Bile (of the liver)	Jupiter
Birth, giving	Pluto
Bladder	Moon
Blood	Pluto co-ruled with Mars and Venus
Blood circulation, cardiovascular system	Sun
Body image	Pluto, Moon, Neptune
Body movements, coordination of	Jupiter

Bone marrow	Saturn
Brain stem	Pluto co-ruled with Uranus and Neptune
Breast milk	Moon
Breasts	Pluto co-ruled with Moon
Bronchial tubes	Uranus
Bursting, physical action of	Uranus
Cancer	Pluto
Capillaries	Pluto co-ruled with Saturn
Cardiovascular system: circulation of the blood	Sun
Cartilage tissues	Saturn with co-ruler Pluto
Cell structure	Saturn
Cells, body – nucleus within	Pluto
Central nervous system	Mercury with co-ruler

	Uranus
Chemoreceptors	Pluto, Venus, Uranus
Chi	Sun
Cholesterol (of the liver)	Jupiter
Cingulate gyros	Moon with Uranus
Communication, within body and to others	Mercury
Connective tissue, loose	Moon with Saturn and Pluto
Consciousness	Neptune
Consciousness of the Soul	Neptune
Co-ordination of the entire body	Jupiter
Cortex	Saturn with Uranus
Corticosterone	Venus with Saturn
Corticotrophin-releasing hormone, or CRH	Venus with Jupiter

Crown chakra	Neptune
Crystallization of various kinds in the body	Saturn
Cutaneous membrane	Saturn
Cutaneous membrane pertaining to the skin	Saturn
Cysts, the formation of	Pluto
Death of the body	Pluto
Decay	Saturn
Dehydration	Uranus
Deposits of various kinds in the body	Saturn
Diseases and infections	Pluto
Dopamine	Uranus
Dreams	Neptune
Duodenum	Pluto co-ruled with Mars
Ear, anatomy of	Mercury

Eliminations	Pluto
Endocrine system	Pluto
Enzymes (all)	Pluto
Esophagus	Mars co-ruled with Pluto
Estrogen	Venus with Pluto
Evolution	Pluto
Eye, smooth muscular tissue	Moon
Eyes	Moon
Fats	Saturn
Feces	Pluto
Feet	Saturn co-ruled with Neptune
Fluids (all) in the body	Neptune with co-rulers Pluto and Moon
Follicle-stimulating hormone (FSH)	Jupiter co-ruled with Saturn, Pluto and Moon

Fornix	Saturn with Uranus
Free radicals	Uranus
Frontal lobes	Venus with Uranus and Neptune
GABA	Uranus co-ruled with Saturn
Gallbladder	Pluto co-ruled with Jupiter
Genetic structures of life itself including humans	Pluto
Gonads (ovaries and testes)	Pluto
Growth hormone (GH)	Jupiter co-ruled with Saturn and Pluto
Growths, out of control, of any kind	Jupiter
Hair	Pluto
Hair follicle receptors	Venus and Pluto

Hallucinations	Neptune
Hands and arms	Mercury
Head	Saturn co-ruled with Mars
Hearing, psychology of	Venus
Heart as an organ	Sun with co-ruler Mars
Heart chakra	Venus
Hepcidin (hormone of the liver)	Jupiter
Hippocampus	Uranus
Hormone secreted from the parathyroid, PTH	Jupiter
Hormones	Pluto
Hormones of the liver	Jupiter
Hormones of the pituitary	Jupiter co-ruled with Saturn and Pluto
Hormones of the thyroid	Jupiter
Hydrocortisone	Venus

hormones, or cortisol	
Hypothalamus	Moon with Uranus and Neptune
Hypothalamus gland	Uranus, Moon, Neptune
Immune system	Neptune
Immune system (intestinal tract)	Neptune with Pluto
Infections and diseases	Pluto
Inner brain	Venus with Neptune and Uranus
Insulin	Pluto
Intestinal tract, entire	Pluto co-ruled with Jupiter
Kidneys	Pluto co-ruled with Venus and Neptune
Kundalini	Pluto
Left hemisphere	Mercury with Uranus

Legs	Saturn co-ruled with Jupiter
Limbic system	Moon with Neptune and Pluto
Liver	Pluto co-ruled with Jupiter
Lungs	Uranus
Luteinizing hormone (LH)	Jupiter co-ruled with Saturn, Mars and Pluto
Lymph glands and tonsils	Pluto co-ruled with Neptune
Mechanoreceptors	Venus
Medulla	Uranus
Melanocyte-stimulating hormone (MSH)	Jupiter co-ruled with Saturn and Pluto
Merkel's disks	Venus and Mercury/Uranus
Messaging within the	Mercury

body	
Messiners corpuscles	Venus and Saturn
Metabolism of all nutrients put into the body	Jupiter
Midbrain	Moon with Uranus
Mitochondria	Pluto
Mold	Pluto
Motor nerves	Mercury
Mucous membranes	Moon with Pluto
Muscle tissue connecting to skeletal bones	Saturn co-ruled with Mars
Muscles	Mars
Muscular tissue of all kinds	Mars
Muscular tissue, smooth, eye	Moon

Mutations	Pluto
Myelin (sheathing within the nerves)	Saturn
Naval chakra	Pluto co-ruled with Mars
Neck	Saturn co-ruled with Venus
Nerve complexes	Uranus and Pluto
Nervous system	Mercury with co-rulers Uranus and Pluto
Neurological disorders	Uranus
Neurons	Uranus
Neurotransmitter serotonin	Moon co-ruled with Saturn
Neurotransmitters	Mercury with Uranus and Neptune
Nociceptors	Venus and Pluto
Nose	Venus with Saturn

Nose, structure of	Saturn co-ruled with Uranus and Venus
Occipital lobe	Moon with Uranus
Oesophagus	Pluto co-ruled with Mars
Optical nerve	Moon
Orbitofrontal cortex	Neptune and Saturn co-rulers with Uranus
Ovaries	Pluto co-ruled with Moon
Ovum	Pluto
Oxytocin	Jupiter with co-ruler Neptune
Pacinian corpuscles	Venus and Pluto
Pancreas (part gland, part organ)	Pluto
Pancreas and liver	Pluto co-ruled with Jupiter
Parahippocampal gyrus	Saturn with Uranus

Parasites	Pluto
Parasympathetic system	Moon with co-rulers Uranus and Mercury
Parathyroid gland	Pluto co-ruled with Saturn and Jupiter
Parietal lobes	Venus with Uranus and Neptune
Pelvis	Saturn with Pluto
Penis	Pluto co-ruled with Mars
Peripheral nervous system	Mercury with co-rulers Uranus and Pluto
Photoreceptors	Venus, Moon, Neptune (higher octave of Venus)
Pimples	Pluto
Pineal gland	Pluto co-ruled with Neptune
Pituitary gland	Pluto co-ruled with Saturn and Jupiter

Placenta	Moon with Neptune and Pluto
Plaque	Pluto
Poisons	Pluto
Posterior pituitary hormones	Jupiter
Prana	Sun
Prefrontal cortex	Uranus with co-rulers Saturn and Mercury
Pregnenolone	Mars
Primary brain	Mars co-ruled with Moon, Uranus and Pluto
Progesterone	Mars
Prolactin	Moon with Jupiter
Prolactin (PRL)	Jupiter co-ruled with Saturn and Pluto
Proprioceptors	Venus and Jupiter

Prostrate, in men	Pluto co-ruled with Jupiter
PTH (hormone secreted from the parathyroid)	Jupiter
Pupil (of the eye)	Moon
Purification	Pluto
Radiation	Pluto
Receptor cells throughout the body	Venus
Receptors in the brain	Venus with Uranus and Neptune
Red blood cells	Mars with Pluto
Regeneration	Pluto
Restrictions of various kinds within the body	Saturn
Retina	Moon
Right hemisphere in the brain	Jupiter

RNA/DNA	Pluto
RNA/DNA, coding of	Pluto
RNA/DNA, messaging of	Mercury
Root chakra, core	Pluto co-ruled with Saturn and Uranus
Root chakra, outer layer	Saturn co-ruled with Uranus
Ruffini's end organs	Venus and Uranus
Sacral chakra	Jupiter with co-ruler Neptune
Sacs	Uranus
Sciatic nerves	Mercury with co-rulers Uranus and Jupiter
Secretions	Pluto
Senses, sensing	Venus and Neptune
Serotonin	Uranus co-ruled with Saturn and Moon
Serotonin	Moon co-ruled with

neurotransmitter	Saturn
Serous membrane	Moon with co-ruler Pluto
Sheath containing myelin	Uranus co-ruled with Saturn
Sheathing within the nerves (myelin)	Saturn
Skeleton (entire)	Saturn
Skin	Saturn with co-ruler Neptune
Skin pigmentation (melanin)	Saturn with co-ruler Neptune
Sleep	Neptune
Soul, consciousness of	Neptune
Sound (produced by vocal cords)	Venus
Sperm	Pluto
Spinal column	Pluto co-ruled with Saturn

Spinal fluid	Saturn co-ruled with Pluto
Spine	Saturn co-ruled with Pluto
Spleen	Pluto co-ruled with Venus and Neptune
Stomach	Pluto co-ruled with Moon
Stress	Uranus
Strokes	Uranus
Structural integrity (overall) of the whole physical body	Saturn
Sympathetic system	Mercury with co-rulers Moon and Uranus
Synapses	Uranus
Synovial fluids	Saturn
Synovial membrane	Saturn with co-ruler Pluto
T cells (from bone marrow)	Saturn

T1 (mono-iodothyronine, hormone of the thyroid)	Jupiter
T2 (di-iodothyronine, hormone of the thyroid)	Jupiter
T3 (tri-iodothyronine or liothyronine, hormone of the thyroid)	Jupiter
T4 (thyroxine, hormone of the thyroid)	Jupiter
Teeth	Saturn
Temperature of the body	Sun
Temporal lobe	Mercury with Uranus
Tension	Uranus
Testes	Pluto co-ruled with Mars
Testosterone	Mars
Thalamus	Uranus with Neptune
Thermoreceptors	Venus, Uranus, Sun

Thinking	Mercury
Third eye chakra	Moon with Pluto
Third eye or ajna chakra	Sun co-ruled with Moon and Pluto
Thought	Mercury
Throat chakra	Mercury
Thrombopoietin (hormone of the liver)	Jupiter
Thymus gland	Pluto co-ruled with Neptune
Thyroid gland	Pluto co-ruled with Jupiter
Thyroid-stimulating hormone (TSH)	Jupiter co-ruled with Saturn and Pluto
Tongue	Venus
Tonsils	Pluto co-ruled with Neptune
Toxins (all)	Pluto

Trachea	Saturn co-ruled with Uranus
Transmissions, internal and external	Mercury
Tumors of all kinds	Pluto
Umbilical cord	Moon with Neptune and Pluto
Urine	Pluto and Moon
Uterus	Pluto co-ruled with Moon
Vagina	Pluto co-ruled with Moon
Valves within the body	Saturn
Valves within the heart	Saturn
Veins	Pluto co-ruled with Mars and Saturn
Viruses	Pluto
Visions	Neptune
Vitality of the body	Sun

Vocal cords	Mercury
Water	Moon with Pluto and Neptune
White blood cells	Venus

OTHER BOOKS ON EVOLUTIONARY ASTROLOGY

PLUTO: THE EVOLUTIONARY JOURNEY OF THE SOUL
(Volume I)
by Jeffrey Wolf Green

Pluto Vol. 1 first went into print in 1984 and has been in continuous print ever since, translated into many languages. It is one of the all-time best selling astrology books. This was the first book in the history of astrology to talk about the Soul and its evolution from life to life. It presented for the first time an actual astrological paradigm that could measure the ongoing evolution of the Soul, a paradigm tested by Jeffrey on over 30,000 clients/souls during his career. Through this work, Jeffrey founded the paradigm of Evolutionary Astrology. He first began lecturing on EA in 1978.

From the time this book exploded onto the scene, over two decades ago, it has continued to set a new pace for the evolution of astrology itself. Jeff Wolf Green's writing embodies everything you would expect from Pluto: intense, powerful, riveting, transformative and penetrating. A book that satiates both the desire for knowledge and the deep yearning for true understanding is a rare find indeed, and just as profound as the information included here, is the deep intuitive awakening it will bring to your own Soul. If you want to help yourself and assist others in conscious evolution, rather than simply waiting for it to happen, this book is the essential map for that journey!

PLUTO: THE SOUL'S EVOLUTION THROUGH RELATIONSHIPS
(Volume II)
by Jeffrey Wolf Green

The second volume details the Soul's evolutionary journey

through relationships of all kinds, and the evolutionary and karmic purposes of such relationships. It discusses the various relationship types, i.e. Karmic, Soul mates, etc., as well as how to apply the EA paradigm in each individual chart to others whom we are in relationship to: synastry. Thus, the evolutionary and karmic background between two Souls can be understood as well as the current life intentions for the relationship itself. The essential needs of any given Soul is discussed as well as the evolutionary and karmic reasons for those needs. A detailed explanation of Venus and Mars is presented in this context.

Additionally, the evolution of a relationship with another(s) is detailed by way of the transiting nature of the core EA paradigm in each individual in the relationship that requires and creates an evolution within the relationship itself. And, finally, the combined Soul in a relationship is focused upon by way of the composite Pluto, the combined Soul, that is seen through the composite chart of any two Souls. This will then correlate to the core evolutionary purpose of the relationship itself. In this chapter, the combined Pluto is presented relative to the natural states of evolution: the consensus, individuated, and spiritual states of evolution.

ESSAYS ON EVOLUTIONARY ASTROLOGY: THE EVOLUTIONARY JOURNEY OF THE SOUL
by Jeffrey Wolf Green
Edited by Deva Green

Deva Green, Jeffrey Wolf Green's daughter, has put together a book that is a compilation of some of Jeffrey's old lectures that have not before appeared in book form. When Jeffrey Wolf Green retired and went into seclusion, he left his daughter Deva with everything that he had ever written which included drafts of various manuscripts which he had intended to publish at various points. This also included every audio tape, video, DVD, and transcript of his lectures delivered over a lengthy career. He also gave Deva his business and asked her to carry on with it. This book reflects her desire to continue to disseminate his work as widely as possible.

Essays on Evolutionary Astrology: The Evolutionary Journey of the Soul, is a combination of transcribed lectures with parts of various manuscripts, most of which has never been in print before. It also includes a vital understanding OF ALL THE PLANETARY NODES IN THE BIRTH CHART.

EVOLUTIONARY ASTROLOGY: PLUTO AND YOUR KARMIC MISSION
by Deva Green

Deva studied EA with her father for many years, from birth in fact. As a result, she is uniquely qualified to carry on his work, which she has been doing since his retirement. Her first book is an in-depth examination of all the core astrological principles that define the Evolutionary Journey of the Soul. Every aspect of the self, from our ambitions and motivations, to the Soul's evolutionary journey, can be traced back to Pluto. This powerful planet of transformation is the key to understanding the factors in your natal chart, ultimately revealing your karmic mission. Inspired by Jeffrey Wolf Green's best-selling, Pluto, Volume I, this groundbreaking astrology book offers clear, step-by-step instruction and practical application of his original work's methods. Pinpoint your Soul's evolutionary intention by locating Pluto in your natal chart. Gain insight into your psychological makeup, identify your Soul's evolutionary stage, and discover your true purpose in this life. Fascinating case studies of famous figures throughout history such as Richard Nixon and Nostradamus lend a vibrant and personal touch to the core principles of Evolutionary Astrology. As you master these techniques, you will reconnect with an evolving sense of purpose and actualize your potential for spiritual growth.

UNDERSTANDING KARMIC COMPLEXES:
Evolutionary Astrology and Regression Therapy
by Patricia Walsh

Patricia is both a graduate of Jeffrey Wolf Green's School of Evolutionary Astrology and a professional past-life regressionist. Patricia has written a groundbreaking book that bridges both disciplines. In it you will find actual past-life histories of individuals, gained through past-life regression techniques, that have the effect of 'proving' the methodology and paradigm of Evolutionary Astrology. It is exceptionally well written. It will help all who seek to understand the paradigm of Evolutionary Astrology learn to correlate the birth chart insights EA reveals with the actual life-to-life experiences that have shaped and conditioned the very nature of the lives that we live, past and present.

INSIGHTS INTO EVOLUTIONARY ASTROLOGY:
A Diverse Collection of Essays by Prominent Astrologers
Edited by Rose Marcus

Evolutionary astrology holds the key to life's most profound mysteries: Where does the Soul come from? How can we grow spiritually? What are our intended life lessons? Shedding new light on these vitally important questions, well-known astrologer Rose Marcus has compiled a collection of illuminating essays by today's foremost evolutionary astrologers, including Jeffrey Wolf Green. Jeffrey Wolf Green, the world-renowned founder of this specialized field of study, begins the book with an exploration of the four natural evolutionary laws that propel Soul growth. Deva Green continues with a discussion of how Pluto drives our evolutionary growth, illustrated with case studies and charts of notable figures such as President Barack Obama. Each contributor offers fascinating perspectives on Evolutionary Astrology and explores various aspects of Pluto's role in determining the Soul's evolving needs and desires. Contributors also explore Pluto's influence on the sexual and relationship characteristics of each zodiacal sign, the fulfillment of human potential, the dynamics between twins, past life regression, the interpretive importance of planetary nodes, and the cultural significance of Pluto entering Capricorn.

URANUS: FREEDOM FROM THE KNOWN
(2014 Revised Edition)
by Jeffrey Wolf Green

Uranus: Freedom from the Known is based on a 6-hour workshop that was given in 1986 by Jeffrey Wolf Green, the founder of Evolutionary Astrology. It focuses primarily on the archetype of liberation from existing inner dynamics that are preventing the evolution of the Soul. Addressed in this book are the archetypes of trauma, individuation, liberation, and de-conditioning. These Uranian archetypes are always in dynamic tension with the

Saturnian archetypes of individual and social conditioning. The dynamic tension between Saturn and Uranus is the primary theme of this book. It is the purpose of Uranus to try to shatter or break free from the conformity patterns that define one's sense of identity, in order to arrive at one's essential unique nature that is unconditioned. Also covered are in-depth descriptions of trauma of the mental, emotional, physical and spiritual bodies correlating to the outer planets; Uranus retrograde, transits, aspects, synastry and composites; and the archetypal correlations of Uranus to anatomy, physiology, and the chakra system, making this one of the most comprehensive 'must-have' books on Uranus from an Evolutionary Astrology point of view. This is a revised and expanded reprinting of the original book that was published in 1986.

NEPTUNE: WHISPERS FROM ETERNITY
by Jeffrey Wolf Green

Neptune: Whispers from Eternity by Jeffrey Wolf Green is a groundbreaking book that explains all the core archetypes that correlate with Neptune, Pisces, and the 12th House. It starts with the core archetypes of consciousness, and the structure of the Soul within consciousness in human form. A specific astrological paradigm is presented that allows the reader to understand the core structure of any Soul's consciousness. The natural evolution of the Soul's consciousness is then discussed relative to the four natural evolutionary states or conditions for it to be within, and how the individual Soul consciousness is given a specific identity in each life by way of the egocentric structure that the Soul creates for its ongoing evolutionary needs.

All the additional core archetypes are discussed such as the inner directions from the Source of the Soul, God/ess, whispers from eternity that attempt to direct the Soul in its evolutionary needs, the sense and need for ultimate meaning in one's life, delusions and illusions, what can be called the 'god complex', deceptions, the collective consciousness and unconsciousness and each individual Soul's relationship to that, various types of instability of the Soul's consciousness such as schizophrenia, dreams and what types, hope and hopelessness, faith, miracles, the various types of wounding of the Soul, purity, innocence, victimization, scapegoating, the power of imagination, psychic phenomena, a discussion of Neptune's lower octave, Venus, and how this correlates to the essential needs of the Soul in relationships, the transit of Neptune in Pisces, and a natural way that is provable to create a super conscious state within yourself that allows for a perception, knowing, of the Manifest and Un-manifested Creation: God.

Each one of these archetypes is exampled by way of birth charts that contributors on the Evolutionary Astrology message board, actual case histories, have submitted that will give you, the reader, a 'hands on' feel and understanding of how to apply Evolutionary Astrology in your own life, the life of your friends and lovers, and your clients if you are a practicing astrologer. There is no other book on Neptune like this one. And, consider this: as you at this very moment are reading these words you are experiencing the 'world' around you as it is. All the events going on in the world, your country, your regions, your city, your group or tribe of like-minded Souls, and your own individual Soul reality within all this.

THIS IS YOUR LIVING EXPERIENCE OF NEPTUNE! THIS IS NEPTUNE'S CONSCIOUSNESS. RIGHT NOW, AND IN EVERY OTHER MOMENT IN TIME. THIS IS THE NATURAL TRIAD OF CONSCIOUSNESS SYMBOLIZED BY THE MOON, YOUR EGO, PLUTO, YOUR SOUL, AND NEPTUNE ITSELF: YOUR INDIVIDUALIZED CONSCIOUSNESS RELATIVE TO THE COLLECTIVE CONSCIOUSNESS OF ALL HUMANS.

STRUCTURE OF THE SOUL
by Jeffrey Wolf Green

The crowning jewel of Jeffrey Wolf Green's body of work is found in his system of chart analysis. His teachings on Pluto and its relationships to the North and South Nodes of Moon, which are commonly referred to as the karmic axis, have completely eclipsed all previous information sources on the subject. This is the very foundation of Evolutionary Astrology which he pioneered. This latest compilation of teachings and discussions from the Jeffrey Wolf Green archives library is a treat for both those who have studied the founder's work, and for students newly embarking on investigation into Evolutionary Astrology.

Chock full of great examples to help you expand your interpretation skills, *Structure of the Soul* provides a review of the Pluto paradigm, the core principles of Evolutionary Astrology, the Nodal Axis of Pluto, and an entire section of the book is dedicated to the Planetary Nodes which provide essential background context that can be easily missed without their inclusion in understanding the evolutionary journey of the Soul. Whether this book is a review or you are coming at it fresh – it is a must read!

LUCIFER: THE INFLUENCE OF EVIL IN THE HORSOCOPE
Jeffrey Wolf Green

This book, Lucifer: The Influence Of Evil In The Horoscope, is based on some lectures that my father had given towards the end of his lengthy career. These lectures have been edited by Adina Mather so that we are able to put them into this form.

My father's desire in shining the light on this influence, and influence that we are all susceptible to, was to help us understand exactly how this influence can manifest in any of our lives. Within this, he also taught that the archetype of Lucifer correlates to the 'Bearer of Light'. In essence, the Lucifer archetype correlates to both the influence of Evil, but also to the influence of the natural God/ess that desires for us to be free of the influence of Evil itself. To do so one must be exactly aware of how the influence of Evil actually exists in our lives. This small book hopefully will do just that.

EA GLOSSARY
(Updated 2015 Edition)
by Jeffrey Wolf Green
Compiled and Edited by Linda Jonson
and The School of Evolutionary Astrology

Incredible EA information, knowledge, wisdom and insight is

skillfully woven into this second edition, condensing Jeffrey Wolf Green's four decades of world-renowned Pluto work into bite-sized info-packets. The EA Glossary is a well-researched, informative and illuminating compilation of key terms, topics and guiding principles used in Jeffrey Wolf Green's Evolutionary Astrology that affirms and expands upon the core EA paradigm taught in his books, *Pluto: The Evolutionary Journey of the Soul (Vol. I)* and *Pluto: The Soul's Evolution through Relationships (Vol. II)*.

Compiled from extracts from the message board of the School of Evolutionary Astrology from March 2009 to December 2014, the EA Glossary provides indispensable study material for resourceful EA students and discerning members of the astrological community, in essence serving as a compass to help navigate into the depths of EA.

EVOLUTIONARY ASTROLOGY: A BEGINNERS GUIDE
by Ari Moshe Wolfe

This book is written for beginners as well as advanced astrology students who are new to the paradigm of Evolutionary Astrology as taught by Jeffrey Wolf Green. It is meant as an aid to those who are interested in studying the teachings of EA as taught by Jeffrey Wolf Green. The core teachings of this book are focused on understanding the nature of the Soul, and how to read the natal chart as a map that describes the reasons for the Soul's current incarnation – all from the point of view of the Soul's ongoing evolutionary journey from life to life.

LILITH: KEEPERS OF THE FLAME
by Mary Blue

This is a story about womankind's natural role as guardians of the Flame of Spirit that dwells within the heart of all human beings. Lilith, the eternal root of the sacred feminine from humankind's spiritual genesis, symbolizes archetypally this role women once held by sacred design and divine intent. They were known as the Keepers of the Flame, those who oversaw and guided the way humans organized themselves in all affairs that governed their lives. The foundation for their way of life was based upon Natural

Law versus man-made laws. One of its core principles was the universal practice of giving, sharing and including. The purpose of this work is to reach out to those who want to go beyond patriarchal conditioning by showing that the history we have been led and taught to believe as true, especially about womankind, is false. In fact, what is true about human nature and its original way of life came before the patriarchy, what is referred to as the matriarchy.

The original archetype of Lilith is described based on the teachings of Jeffrey Wolf Green with the intent to help bolster and invigorate every woman's spirit by showing her the way back home to her own natural self; to stand again as one individual who exists as part of a group consciousness, the species human, interwoven into an even larger family comprised of all Earth's sacred beings, and by doing so, to reconnect to the Spirit that dwells within each and every heart linking all to her own, and to relearn how to speak its Truths with passion and conviction for the benefit of all. That is Lilith.

You will know truth when it speaks to your soul. It is a knowingness that simply exists beyond the words. As I read through the book, I felt an immediate resonance with the concepts put forth by the author. I learned, I absorbed, I embraced. Somehow I remembered. The remembering felt as natural as breath in, breath out. Great educators like Carl Jung and Joseph Campbell have described how ancient myths continue to inform and live on within our collective unconscious. Our great spiritual teachers, many of whom are referenced within the pages of this book, remind each one of us of our connection to universal source, to the divinity that exists within each one of us. They invite us to embark on the journey inward, to reconnect with our center, our soul, and with the source of all that is.

In this luminous book, the author exquisitely and simply synthesizes the knowledge imparted by the spiritual masters regarding our Creatress force. She speaks of the transgender whole of the sacred feminine in its unfiltered and unconditioned version. This is not the Lilith story with the overlay of patriarchal conditionings that give an explanation for humanity's spiritual downfall, but rather that of her preHerstory - of the unified, fecund and regenerative Creatress seed from which all life has sprung. I invite you to allow your own knowingness to verify the truth contained within these pages. Don't read this book - experience it, for yourself, for your soul.

Rose Marcus
Evolutionary Astrologer,
Author, "Insights into Evolutionary Astrology"

All of the above books are available from many sources but can also be purchased from the School of Evolutionary Astrology website. If you are interested in becoming a Certified Evolutionary Astrologer, there is a comprehensive DVD course available. This is based on the very first School that Jeffrey Wolf Green taught in Evolutionary Astrology. For further information, please visit the website:

www.schoolofevolutionaryastrology.com

AUDIO CDs AND WORKSHOP TRANSCRIPTS

Audio CDs

- Evolutionary Astrology and Sexuality
- Evolutionary Astrology and the Influence of Lucifer
- Evolutionary Astrology and The Planetary Method of Chart Interpretation
- Metamorphosis and the Ascendant
- Evolutionary Astrology and the Mars/Pluto Interface
- Saturn and Evolutionary Astrology
- Evolutionary Astrology: Synastry and Composite Charts
- The Search for Inner Meaning: The Triad of the 12th, 7th, and 2nd Houses
- Evolutionary Astrology and Venus: Issues In Relationship
- Astrology and the Chakras

Workshop Transcripts

- Astrology and the Chakra System
- A Seminar of Lectures on Uranus and Neptune
- A Seminar of Two Lectures:
- Pluto: The Evolutionary Cause of Incarnation
- Saturn/Neptune and the Nature of Divine Discontent
- Astrology and Sexuality
- The Moon Workshop
- The 8th House: Gateway to Self-Realization
- Aspects, Phases, and Key Planetary Pairs
- The Progressed Moon
- Uranus Workshop: Freedom from the Known
- Neptune Workshop
- How to Spiritualize Your Life
- Transits, Progressions, and Solar Returns
- Workshop on Careers
- Evolutionary Transitions
- The Fifth House
- The Planets
- Karmic and Evolutionary Astrology

- The Signs: A Seminar of Four Lectures from Holland
  - Pluto: The Evolutionary Journey of the Soul
  - The Saturn/Neptune Conjunction: The Nature of Divine Discontent
  - Trauma and the Outer Planets
  - Mercury and the Nature of Thought
- So We Meet Again, Eh?
- A Three Lecture Seminar
  - Parent/Child Dynamics
  - The Planetary Nodes
  - Retrograde Planets
- All About Saturn
- Issues in Self-Improvement: The 6th House
- A Planetary Method of Chart Interpretation
- Neptune and its Archetypal Meaning in the Horoscope

For further information and to order:

www.schoolofevolutionaryastrology.com/school/ea-transcripts-for-purchase

DVDs FOR SALE ON AMAZON

CYCLES OF BECOMING

In this over 4 hour long class Jeffrey teaches about the evolutionary nature of the 360 degree circle; the eight archetypal lunation cycles within it such as the New Phase, Crescent Phase, and so on; all the aspects that take place within the phases and how they evolve; and key planetary pairs that operate in all birth charts archetypally such as the Sun and Moon, the Moon and Saturn, Mars and Venus, and so on. If you truly desire to understand the evolutionary nature of all these dynamics this DVD is for you.

A PLANETARY METHOD OF CHART INTERPRETATION

In this over 4 hour long class Jeffrey teaches his unique planetary method of chart calculation that is used in Evolutionary Astrology. This method is used in relationship to the core Evolutionary Paradigm that exists within all birth charts: natal Pluto, its polarity point, the North and South Nodes of the Moon, and the location of their planetary rulers. This method is then used in a step by step manner starting with the Sun, and then all the other planets sequentially. In this way a core understanding as to the WHY of any planet being in whatever sign and house is understood as what the Soul desires and needs for its ongoing evolutionary journey.

THE MOON

In this comprehensive 90 minute class Jeffrey teaches about ALL of the archetypes that correlate with the Moon, Cancer, and the 4th house, and how to apply them to your astrological work.

FROM KARMA TO DHARMA

In this incredibly in-depth 4 hour long class Jeffrey first reviews in tremendous depth the core Evolutionary Paradigm that exists within all birth charts which symbolizes the ongoing evolutionary journey of the Soul from life to life, but then teaches about the natural polarity points of all planets in the birth chart that correlate to the evolutionary truth of the Soul, DHARMA or TRUTH, that when consciously embraced by the Soul metamorphoses the KARMA that the Soul has brought into the current life. This is the only time that Jeffrey taught about this. It is a must for all those who desire to understand evolutionary astrology in the most total way possible.

PLUTO: THE EVOLUTIONARY JOURNEY OF THE SOUL

In this 240 minute class Jeffrey teaches in total detail about the nature of the revolutionary/evolutionary nature of the Evolutionary Paradigm that exists in all birth charts: Pluto, its polarity point, the North and South Nodes of the Moon, and the location of their planetary rulers. He teaches about the evolutionary nature of the aspects with the birth chart, the four natural evolutionary states for the Soul, the three ways that the Soul effects its evolutionary intentions, and the nature of 'skipped steps' in the Soul's evolutionary journey, how to identify them, and how to resolve them. He also teaches about transits, and what they mean in the evolutionary progression of the Soul in the current life it is living.

THE PLANETS

Jeffrey teaches in extensive detail about the archetypal correlations to all the planets, and how to understand and apply them to your astrological work.

THE PLANETARY NODES

In this four hour DVD Jeffrey Wolf Green teaches about the nature and function of all the Planetary Nodes in the birth chart. All planets have a North and South Node. Thus, each natal planet has its own Nodal Axis that correlates to a Natural Trinity within the birth chart that correlates to the past archetypes, the South Node, that the Soul has been using for its ongoing evolutionary journey, the North Node which correlate to where the Soul is evolving towards, and the Natal Planet which correlates with how the Past and the Future are integrated in each moment throughout life. Jeffrey Wolf Green was the first evolutionary astrologer who taught about the importance of including the Nodes of the planets in the birth chart that correlate with the ongoing evolutionary journey of the Soul from life to life. This is an extensive teaching of how to understand and apply the Planetary Nodes to the natal birth chart.

CAPRICORN: THE NATURE OF DARK EROS

In this 90 minute class Jeffrey teaches about the nature of sexual desires that when repressed become the basis of distortion and rage that manifests itself in all kinds of ways: dark Eros. Within this he teaches about natural sexual laws that have themselves become distorted due to the nature of patriarchal conditioning which starts with the invented religions of men.

SO WE MEET AGAIN, EH?

Jeffrey teaches about how most of the people that we come into some kind of intimate contact with in the current life we have had some sort of prior life connection to. This includes friends, lovers, parents, children. He then teaches how to understand the karmic and evolutionary dynamics between any two people through the use of synastry and composite charts.

THE LAST PUBLIC TALK BY JEFFREY WOLF GREEN

This is a DVD of the very last time Jeffrey Wolf Green lectured or talked in public. This two DVD set took place at one of his conferences on Evolutionary Astrology held in Sedona, Arizona, in 2004. In it he sits on stage and answers the many and varied questions from the large audience about various topics within the totality of the Evolutionary Astrology paradigm that he pioneered starting in 1977.

All the above DVDs are available for purchase at
www.amazon.com.
(Type Jeffrey Wolf Green DVDs in the search-bar.)

EVOLUTIONARY ASTROLOGY AUTHORS AND TRANSLATORS

The Jeffrey Wolf Green School of Evolutionary Astrology is now offering to publish new authors of Jeffrey Wolf Green's Evolutionary Astrology paradigm under its banner.

If you are an author who is writing a subject that is rooted and based on the Evolutionary Astrology paradigm and would like the School to publish your book, please contact us for further information.

The Jeffrey Wolf Green School of Evolutionary Astrology needs people who can translate the various books on Evolutionary Astrology into other languages.

These books will be published by the School and sold on Amazon.com through all their international sites around the world, and in local bookstores in any country.

For further information on becoming an EA Author or Translator, please contact:

eaastro@schoolofevolutionaryastrology.com

Jeffrey Wolf Green Evolutionary Astrology

Become a Certified Evolutionary Astrologer

JEFFREY WOLF GREEN

School of Evolutionary Astrology

DVD COURSE

The original Evolutionary Astrology Pluto School taught by founder, Jeffrey Wolf Green, in Arizona—1994

www.schoolofevolutionaryastrology.com

MEDICAL ASTROLOGY

Sanicle tincture → constipation
① or ♀ transit
P65 Licorice root — Osteoporosis — Herb
63 Sun 11.H. Blindness + Stroke
    MS — lipoic acid 200mg daily + magnesium + calcium
    Debilitating DEPRESSION:
    Valerian, Pulsatilla, ignatia
65 Mental instability → 4,☉, 11.H, ☿,♃, 12.H.
61 Migraines

42 ☉ = Security driven
43 5HTP — restoring brain
44 Lung formula
46 Bloodsugar Sanicle (herb)
47 Colitis — Sanicle, catnip
    Eczema
49 Pluto transit 4.H. — 5-HTP
52 Dreams Valerian, Gotu Kola

(77) for me + (79)
① ♆ — stressful traumatic Event in the past
♂ Bloodflow + men genitalia

Pg 97 ♂♀☿ Drinking plenty of water to keep the serotonin level up, which would keep them calm —
Article — "Trauma + the outer Planets"

Made in the USA
Middletown, DE
30 June 2018